ADVENTURES ON THE CHINA WINE TRAIL

ADVENTURES ON THE CHINA WINE TRAIL

How Farmers, Local Governments, Teachers, and Entrepreneurs Are Rocking the Wine World

Cynthia Howson and Pierre Ly

ROWMAN & LITTLEFIELD
Lanham • Boulder • New York • London

Published by Rowman & Littlefield
An imprint of The Rowman & Littlefield Publishing Group, Inc.
4501 Forbes Boulevard, Suite 200, Lanham, Maryland 20706
https://rowman.com

6 Tinworth Street, London SE11 5AL, United Kingdom

British Library Cataloguing in Publication Information Available

Library of Congress Control Number: 2019951692

9781538133521 (cloth : alk. paper) | 9781538133538 (epub)

♾ ™ The paper used in this publication meets the minimum requirements of American National Standard for Information Sciences Permanence of Paper for Printed Library Materials, ANSI/NISO Z39.48-1992.

CONTENTS

ACKNOWLEDGMENTS

We could fill volumes with the people who made the last six years possible, so we apologize to those we will inevitably miss. First, we thank everyone we encountered in the Chinese wine industry. Their generosity brought not only the entirety of this book but also time, friendship, food, laughter, logistical help, and more.

Several of those we worked with became such good friends that we fly to visit whenever we're in China. Zhang Yanzhi, Liao Zusong, Liu Jianjun, Snow, and Hermas Huang are the ones who keep us returning to Ningxia and Fuzhou, even when the research doesn't precisely require it. One more name on that list brings lumps to our throats with the smiles on our faces. The late, generous, kind, loving, inspiring Indiana Jones of Chinese wine, Gérard Colin, brought immeasurable joy and insight to our work. He died unexpectedly, with a glass of wine, doing what he loved.

Jeff Begun was our coauthor during our first fieldwork visit in 2013. His exuberance, friendship, fearlessness, and love of language and China brought joy as well as phone numbers, research assistants, and our first adventures.

Our research assistants are professional interpreters whose tireless skill in multiple languages has astounded us. That contribution is the tip of the iceberg. They build bridges, provide cultural insight, smooth out errors, and translate not only words but also the emotional content behind the words. These young scholars taught us to make every visit the most fun learning experience we could have. Thank you, Josephine Mao, Yunshan Niu, Joyce Zhang, Dora Zhou, Christy Ouyang, and Chloe Chen.

Key experts gave us the early insights and contacts we needed to know what questions to ask and where the story might take us: Judy Chan, Ma Huiqin, Zhang Jing, Jim Sun and Sarah Chen, Fongyee Walker, Brendan Galipeau, Lu Yang, Jim Boyce, and Liz Thach.

Dozens more winemakers, farmers, teachers, and entrepreneurs made our work possible: Professor Zhou Shuzhen, Crazy Fang, Wu Hongfu, Mr. Ma and his son George, Emma Gao, and Thierry Courtade in Ningxia; Zhuge, Hongxing, Gavin Cui, Luciano Vera, and everyone in Adong village in Yunnan; professors at the College of Enology in Yangling: Li Hua, Wang Hua, Fang Yulin, Li Jiagui, Liu Shuwen, Li Huanmei, Denise Cosentino, Alessio Fortunato, and their students; Wang Zheng at Jade Valley; Eddie McDougall, aka The Flying Winemaker, in Hong Kong.

Our friend and mentor, Mike Veseth, not only saw our future in wine research but also paved the way that made it possible. The master of constant but discreet guidance, Mike nudged us toward wine research in the first place, introduced us to our first contacts and our editor, and advised us personally and professionally throughout the process. Together, Mike and Sue Veseth have read chapters and provided wine, food, wisdom, and secrets from the worlds of wine and writing.

Gordon and Sonia Trimble generously funded several trips through the Charles Garnet Trimble Fund and graciously hosted us during our exchange program in Fuzhou. Thanks to Sean Wang for our stay in Fuzhou and making us want to come back. The University of Puget Sound and University of Washington Tacoma provided funding, research support, and the professional environment that make our work what it is. Mimi Martin, from the Wines and Spirits Archive, taught us about wine and trusted us to lead blind tastings with her students. Edouard Cointreau provided invaluable advice and networking opportunities through the Gourmand Awards.

Our first book demanded immeasurable patience from our editor, Susan McEachern; Katelyn Turner; Janice Braunstein; copy editors; and the entire team at Rowman & Littlefield. Our book proposal benefited from the unexpected help and generosity of natural wine superstar, Alice Feiring.

The American Association of Wine Economists connected us to an entire community of wine researchers who have made our work better and much more fun: Raphaël Schirmer helped us understand maps of China; Haiyan Song hosted us at Hotel ICON; and Javier Merino, Aldo and Mariano Biondolillo, and Nick Vink helped us explore land, grapes, and the political economy of wine.

Our parents, families, friends, and colleagues around the world helped, read, encouraged, tolerated, ran, tasted, hugged, and made us who we are.

1

FROM CHINA TO BORDEAUX . . . AND BACK

It wasn't long into our first Chinese winery visit when our friendly guide in uniform gave up, realizing she had promised far more than she could handle. Back at the ticket office, she had kindly offered the English version of the tour. No problem, she thought, as her colleague gave her a thick stack of pages and we walked through the turnstile entrance, our colorful tickets in hand. But you see, reading a script in English aloud when you don't speak the language is very, very hard. After an honorable effort filled with apologetic giggles, she mimed the solution: she would continue walking along to get us to each stop in proper order, while Cynthia took over the reading.

We'll never forget our Chinese wine tourism debut at Changyu AFIP, an easy day trip north of Beijing. A stunning wine amusement park, complete with faux-French castles, a European-style village, cafés, a church, tennis courts, a museum, and, of course, vineyards and a winery. It was beautiful, surreal, and bizarrely empty. But the genius of such a place is to entertain Grandma and the kids, even if they don't like wine.

Of course, we do like wine, so when our guide pointed to the royal tasting room, we were excited. We'd read all about Chinese wine but had never tried any. A few months earlier, the prospect of connecting wine with our research on economic development was enough for us to block off part of the summer and buy nonrefundable flights to China, where we'd never been. At last, our China wine adventure had begun. We sat in the comfortable chairs and our samples arrived.

European-style chateau at Changyu AFIP, near Beijing.

Oh my. What had we done? The 2008 Chardonnay was drinkable, though probably far too old. And the 2005 Cabernet Sauvignon (if that's what it was) smelled, well, problematic. Why would they choose to serve these wines to visitors? Isn't the tasting room supposed to make you want more? But we had hope for the following weeks. The faux-French castle combined with questionable wine was an iconic image of wine made in China that we'd seen in French and American news stories. But things were changing fast, and these two wines were remnants from another era. Even state-owned giant Changyu makes critically acclaimed wines now, and they may be closer to you than you think. Let's start over, farther inland.

* * *

Oozing pep, Wang Fang practically skipped as she led us through her winery, Kanaan, near Yinchuan, the capital of Ningxia Hui Autonomous Region. We'd met a week earlier at a wine expo near the Great Wall, where her zingy dry Riesling caught our attention. Kanaan wines were on a roll. A few months earlier, British wine critic extraordinaire Jancis

Robinson had attended a blind tasting of Chinese wines, singling out Kanaan's 2011 Cabernet Sauvignon–Merlot blend as "the wine that I thought was best of all."[1] Known as "Crazy Fang" among friends and colleagues, our host's foray into the wine business was more recent than you'd think.

She was still living in Germany when her father suggested she come home and invest in a new winery. She knew nothing about the business or production of wine, but life in Germany had confirmed an important prerequisite: "I like to drink." She also trusted her father was on to something, with good reason. In 2005, starting his retirement, he cofounded Helan Qingxue, the Ningxia winery whose 2009 red wine made a big splash in the wine world when it won Best Bordeaux Varietal over £10 at the 2011 Decanter World Wine Awards. In his drive to convince her to get in the game, he may have been less clear about certain details. When she asked him about cost, he estimated she would need to invest two to three million yuan (about three to five hundred thousand US dollars) to get started. It turned out to be far more expensive. "I'll never trust him again," she joked. But in hindsight, you can't deny the elder's vision. By 2010, tanks and barrels were up and running to produce the first vintage, and now Kanaan is widely recognized as one of China's best wineries.

Wait a second. What are we talking about here? Wine made in . . . China? Most people we meet are dubious at the mere mention of Chinese wine, even when they didn't know there was such a thing, let alone having ever tried it. They may love the food, the teas, and even their Lenovo tablets. But wine? No, thanks! Writers have left a trail of memorable tasting notes. At worst, your Chinese wine may be reminiscent of "ashtray, coffee grounds and urinal crust," like the first one Mike Veseth (the *Wine Economist*) tasted. Or, in the words of a wine journalist, it could have "a smell of baked dead mouse!" We'll leave it up to you to decide which one sounds worse.[2]

Until recently, for most people, at best, Chinese wine didn't exist. At worst, they had read the tasting notes, or tried a bad one during a China trip. So imagine the world's surprise when the 2011 Decanter World Wine Awards were announced. That couldn't be real. It couldn't be that Chinese wine, well, tasted good. There had to be a better explanation, because otherwise it could be the start of something all too familiar by now. First it was socks and T-shirts, then steel, and next thing we knew, Chinese cell phones, laptops, and even solar panels were everywhere. So, the fact that China was regularly listed as one of the top ten wine-producing countries by volume in the world sounded familiar too. But is it true? Over the years, estimates have shifted and experts have questioned the numbers, but China's wine production has been large enough to stun international observers for more than a decade. Could China take over the wine world as well?

What is it about China that makes so many people skeptical about its wine potential? Try bringing up the wines of Georgia or Brazil with people who know nothing about them. They may be surprised, but chances are they won't be worried about you for drinking them. By contrast, look at what happened when Helan Qingxue won the Decanter Award. Skeptics went as far as to question not just the authenticity of the wine (was it French wine with a Chinese label?) but also the integrity of *Decanter* magazine, suggesting an ulterior business motive in awarding the gold medal.[3] Wine writer Jaime Goode deleted his own coverage of the event because the comment thread "got messy and it upset people."[4] From reading all this, you could have assumed a major diplomatic incident occurred. But no, it really was just about wine.

All the skepticism and incredulity around Chinese wine may have something to do with parts of the broader "Made in China" image that have stuck to the wine. After all, the country's reputation for counterfeiting and food safety scandals may have tainted the idea of Chinese wine from the start.

And yet, here we are. As blogger Jim Boyce puts it, in only a decade, the wine world has gone from asking whether good Chinese wine was even possible, on to searching for the best ones, and now to discussing which wines are more interesting or a better value for the money.[5] By wine standards, that's very fast. Kanaan is one of many up-and-coming Chinese wineries that have helped change the idea of Chinese wine. And it hasn't been an easy task.

What happened? How did we get from largely ignoring the idea of wine made in China to gold medals and praise by famous critics in less than a decade? In this book, we take you along our adventures on the China wine trail to meet the farmers, entrepreneurs, and teachers who are rocking the wine world. Maybe, just maybe, there's nothing to be scared about after all. We will travel to Chinese wine tourism hot spots and show you how much fun they can be, sometimes in a weird sort of way. We will talk to winemakers who face no shortage of headaches in their quest to get their hands on good wine grapes. We will take you to green, lush mountains at such high elevation that your shampoo bottle might explode, and then to a desert, to see what French multinational corporations have in common with small Chinese farms. Then, it will be time to go back to school—Chinese wine school, of course—to meet teachers, and their students eager to join the wine workforce. And in case you travel to China but really can't make it to the wineries, we'll reveal where we bought those local wines we love, and even where we found them on the menu by the glass. Finally, we'll tell you what happened when we subjected thirsty participants to blind tastings of Chinese wines. And what if, soon, you could buy some closer to home, even if you never make it to the Middle Kingdom?

Our choices of stories, wines, and destinations were often shaped by what time and budget allowed, as well as serendipitous encounters. We don't pretend to provide a comprehensive list. But we hope that our stories will make you curious about Chinese wines, help you understand the people behind them, and be a starting point for your own China wine adventures.

* * *

That morning at Kanaan, a friend of Fang's joined our little group. The man knew his way around a cellar. Our host understandably ignored us for a while to seek his comments on every aspect of the wines and equipment. After our round of tasting barrel samples, Mr. Guest Expert said goodbye and walked out to the parking lot. Happy to catch her attention again, we mentioned our interest in meeting people on the sales and distribution side of the business. "You should talk to him!" She ran to catch him outside. Our name cards exchange on the sunny front porch was brief but memorable. "J'étais représentant pour Petrus en Chine," he said, introducing himself in fluent French. "On pourra se parler à mon bureau à Pékin." Zhang Yanzhi built his successful business, Easy Cellar, on something that China has been much better known for worldwide than making wine: drinking it.

But the wine boom is recent. While China is the fifth-largest wine-consuming country in the world,[6] wine consumption per capita is still very small.[7] China does drink, a lot, but according to a World Health Organization report, wine represented just 3 percent of consumption of alcoholic beverages in 2010. Beer amounted to almost ten times that. And the lion's share, more than two-thirds, was (and still is) stronger stuff: distilled spirits.[8] In fact, one of the first and largest Chinese wineries began at least as much because of wine as for selling a very famous French brand of Cognac. The brand made it to the odd news section a few years ago, with the story of a certain Ms. Zhao.

It was about noon on August 21, 2015, when Ms. Zhao's flight landed in Beijing after a long, straight journey from the United States. She must have been looking forward to showing off the nice bottle of French Cognac she'd bought after security at an American airport and safely tucked in her carry-on luggage. With only a brief layover before boarding again for her hometown, Wenzhou, she had to be efficient. We had to do this kind of short layover a few times, so we know the feeling. With her luggage safely checked all the way home, Ms. Zhao's turn at this last checkpoint finally came. But there was bad news. Her bottle of Cognac, which cost her almost two hundred dollars, was over the one-hundred-milliliter limit for liquids allowed in carry-on luggage. She had to give it away to security, the officer informed. What would you do in this situation? Would you try to beg your way out of this? Transfer some parts of it into one of your empty TSA-compliant shampoo bottles?

There is no negotiating with airport security. So, Ms. Zhao went a different route: to avoid wasting the precious liquor, she opened the bottle and chugged it.[9] Yes, it sounds ill advised, but it wasn't just any Cognac. It was Rémy Martin's XO Excellence.

She won't have trouble replacing it, though it's unclear whether she'll ever want to after this. The China journey of Rémy Martin, one of France's leading Cognac producers, took a modern turn in 1980, soon after China began opening to the rest of the world. In 1979, to attract foreign investors, the country passed its first Joint Venture Law. To develop domestic industries, the government welcomed new investors but made sure to keep them on a tight leash by placing limits on foreigners' equity shares, rules governing the distribution of profit, or targeting strategic sectors. Rémy Martin seized the opportunity and formed a partnership with the city of Tianjin. The resulting joint venture, one of the first in the country in any sector, was Dynasty Fine Wines.

For Rémy Martin, the point was not to outsource production of Cognac made more cheaply in China. Cognac must come from Cognac in southwestern France, and that's a large part of its brand and appeal. On the wine side, some Dynasty dry rosé was exported to the United States, at a time when one of the winery's main grape sources was a farm staffed by prison labor. Still, that didn't start a major Chinese wine boom. Even now, few investors dream of making Chinese wine for export, so back in 1980, that was probably not Rémy's intention either.

Helping to make local wine was really a foot in the door to a huge potential new market for Cognac. Over the years, Cognac became a classic luxury gift. Ironically, business went so well in China that after the 2013 crackdown on corruption and lavish entertainment expenses by government officials, Rémy Cointreau (the group's corporate name since 1991) reported a significant decline in sales because of its heavy exposure in the Chinese market.[10]

Dynasty got a great deal too. Although it is struggling today, the winery has long been one of the Chinese wine giants, along with Changyu, Great Wall, and Dragon Seal. On its website, the company plays up its association with Rémy Cointreau, credited for having "introduced and applied its sophisticated skills in wine production and profound industry knowledge to fully support Dynasty." In 2011, when Robert Parker's colleague, Lisa Perrotti-Brown, published the magazine's first ratings of twenty Chinese wines, Dynasty was included as one of only three producers for this tasting, along with acclaimed smaller producers Grace Vineyard and Silver Heights. Dynasty was well represented, including two sparkling wines, two whites, and two reds, scoring between 74 and 81 points, that is, "average" to "barely above average." Not bad, commentators noted, especially as the reputation of Chinese wine abroad was either nonexistent or very poor.[11]

What happened to Ms. Zhao, by the way? Seconds after chugging the bottle in front of baffled security officers and travelers, she started rolling on the floor, screaming uncontrollably. Concerned for her safety and that of her fellow passengers, security staff decided boarding was out of the question. They put her in a wheelchair and took her to an airport lounge to receive medical attention. She woke up seven hours later, thanked the team, and family members took her home. The story doesn't say whether she ever replaced that bottle.

Distilled spirits continue to dominate the alcoholic beverages market in China, eclipsing wine by miles. And among distilled spirits, while Cognac is a very successful import, the fiery Chinese grain liquor Baijiu still represents the vast majority of the market.

This very popular high-octane drink has been a mainstay of Chinese celebrations forever. Government officials spent their entertainment budgets on expensive Baijiu to impress guests, and the whole party would drink itself into a coma. Many foreign businesspeople tell stories about their Baijiu-filled dinners in China. In the 1990s, with China's growing population and wealth, the government became concerned about Baijiu consumption for two reasons. Beyond health (reason number one) was the fact that Baijiu production takes precious grain away from the food supply. In 1996, as the idea of wine having health benefits grew, Chinese premier Li Peng encouraged people to switch: "Drinking fruit wines is helpful to our health, does not waste grain, and is good for social ethics." From then on, red wine was served at official banquets, and local wine production became increasingly encouraged. [12]

* * *

Entering university in 1995, Zhang Yanzhi joined the second graduating class of a then fledgling winemaking program near Xi'an, at a time when interest in wine was rare. There were ten professors teaching just twenty-eight students. But how did he get into wine in the first place? We assumed his choice of college major came from falling in love with a taste. Was there a specific bottle, at a family dinner, that gave him the wine bug? Were his parents into wine? That's not at all what happened. It turns out he didn't choose to study wine. God did that for him, he said. Well, maybe it was the hand of God, but through the peculiarities of the Chinese higher-education system. Have you heard of Gaokao, the ridiculously difficult end-of-high-school exams that determine Chinese kids' entrance into university, and perhaps even their future professional success? Try to write an eight-hundred-word essay on the following question from a 2013 exam: "The containers for milk are always square boxes; containers for mineral water are always round bottles; round wine bottles are usually placed in square boxes. Write a composition on the subtle philosophy of the round and square." [13]

Yanzhi grew up in a modest household in Shandong Province. His parents were farmers. For him, as for millions of kids, entrance into one of the few top Chinese universities represented a ticket to a better life. He had a plan: he would go to a university program for police and military work, a highly sought-after route back then, with seats available for only one student per province each year. Students from Yanzhi's generation had even less choice than today. The government selected students for each program based on their scores and other factors. His high Gaokao performance was more than enough to earn him the coveted spot, but the next guy in Shandong won the placement, and there was a hint that family connections played a role. Somehow, the government ended up sending him to the new but promising viticulture and enology program near Xi'an.

After graduation, he worked as a cellar assistant at Changyu, China's gigantic and oldest winery. In 2002, he decided to pursue more advanced wine training where one of his Chinese professors had graduated: the prestigious wine program at the University of Bordeaux, which he could attend thanks to a scholarship from the Académie du Vin de Bordeaux. The first year was tough. He had to repeat it, as he struggled with the language. But he embraced French culture and has fond memories of his time there. During one internship in the Médoc region, he lived with a family, sharing their meals and sleeping in their son's room. With his French all caught up, Yanzhi qualified for year 2 of the Diplôme national d'œnologue. As if it wasn't enough, he completed a concurrent master's degree in wine business law, economics, and management. And it was in Bordeaux that he met his wife, another Chinese student, enrolled at Bordeaux University's school of architecture.

Back to the homeland, boosted by the cachet of a Bordeaux wine education, he spent a few years working for a major Chinese wines and spirits group, on matters having little to do with winemaking. The company bet that his French skills and professional contacts would open doors for new property acquisitions, and later for marketing their various brands. Hankering to reconnect with wine, he convinced the boss to give him a shot at heading the group's winery. But the group's idea of wine was just too different from his. Two years later, after a week pondering what he really wanted to do, he was gone.

Soon, the paperwork to create his wine import business, Easy Cellar, was in the pipeline, but it went dormant for a while as another exciting opportunity came along. When Établissements Jean-Pierre Moueix, a major Bordeaux wine merchant, needed a good China representative for the group's wines, they knew who to call. During his studies in Bordeaux in 2005, Yanzhi had interned at the family's flagship property, legendary Pomerol producer Chateau Petrus, and made friends with the company's president, Christian Moueix. A few years later, when Moueix called, it was the last quarter of a very special year in wine. The year 2009 was immediately hyped as the "vintage of the century" for Bordeaux producers, when the weather did everything just right for the wines to be praised by top critics. You can learn all about the 2009 vintage story in *Red Obsession*, a documentary film about the Bordeaux China wine connection, narrated by Russell Crowe. Thanks to demand from wealthy Chinese enthusiasts, Bordeaux's top wines sold for record prices. And since fine wine of that caliber is not just a drink but also an investment, speculation ensued. It was the peak of a wine boom era, driven not yet by regular Chinese consumers getting into it for the taste but by status and gifting. Wealthy elites and government officials with big entertainment budgets sought the most famous wines to impress business guests. Bordeaux weather played nice again in 2010, leading producers to raise their prices even more. But by summer 2011, the year Yanzhi agreed to be a wine expert for the first-ever wine investment fund in China, it became clear that prices had gotten out of hand. The Bordeaux bubble in China started to make a hissing sound.

In 2012, Yanzhi decided it was time to get Easy Cellar out of hibernation. It must have been an interesting year to try and fly on his own in the wine trade. "It was the crisis of Bordeaux wine in China," he remembered. "It's a bit better now." That November, China's new president, Xi Jinping, announced unprecedented anticorruption measures to crack down on bribes and tame government officials' luxurious habits. A recent study by Yale economists found that while the kind of consumption that could easily be hidden from the public remained, more visible luxury goods imports fell by almost 55 percent.[14] Everybody felt it: taxi drivers, luxury hotels, and, of course, wine merchants. Gone were the days when money seemed to be no object. And it wasn't just hard for imports. Many Chinese wineries, too, had been riding the wave, some even selling much of their production at very high prices to government officials. Some observers rejoiced. Perhaps the earlier boom had been a mirage, having little to do with people's actual taste for wine. With the highest-margin sales coming to an end, wine merchants would finally target a class of regular consumers interested in wine for the taste and demanding value for the money. Free-trade agreements with Chile and Australia promised to make good-value wine increasingly available, and Chinese wineries would have to compete.

Today, Yanzhi has a network of distributors who sell the wines he imports. But in the early days of Easy Cellar, he didn't have a lot of contacts yet. Big foreign-invested importers were very good at selling their wine portfolios through public channels such as shops and restaurants, so competing with them would have been tough. Instead, he first focused on a private channel, a game he thought small Chinese importers like him were better placed to play than the big guys. He sold high-end wines to serious (and wealthy) wine enthusiasts, the kind of people who prefer to use their personal contacts to find wine sources they can trust. Imagine you need a bottle of a famous wine for your collection, or to impress guests at a business dinner. You could go to a shop, but with all the news about counterfeiting going around, can you trust what you're buying? Yanzhi's clients trusted him, thanks to his Bordeaux credentials, French fluency, and relationships with big names in the wine world. And he could provide good-value offerings too, importing a hundred or so different labels, including reasonably priced Bordeaux and Spanish producers. For sparkling wine, he chose to focus on the more affordable Spanish cava, instead of Champagne.

While this approach worked, he felt limited. Everything was so individualized that it was hard to grow. With a changing market increasingly populated by consumers in search of good wine at good prices, Yanzhi chose to focus more on global brands. During the earlier wine boom, many importers sought to get exclusive deals with foreign wineries that even made special labels only sold in China. Yanzhi saw a growing demand for wines sold with the label they were known for worldwide. His portfolio now includes a range of price points and brands, such as Australia's Penfolds wines, South Africa's Glennelly Estate, Napa Valley's Dominus, French Côtes du Rhone brand Les Dauphins, and of course, several Bordeaux wines. To this day, he remains on excellent terms with Moueix and still carries some of the group's wines. These wines don't sell themselves. With his team, he hosts countless wine dinners for his distributor clients all around China and even takes them to visit the wine regions, all expenses paid, to turn them into good brand ambassadors.

It must help that over the last decade, consumers and professionals have become more knowledgeable about wine. With the growing taste for drinking and selling it, the drive to learn more has fueled an expanding market for wine education. Of course, we couldn't wait to visit the schools.

* * *

As we often did before we finally bought smartphones and Pierre figured out how to use the Chinese equivalent of Google Maps, we got lost in the maze of high-rise office buildings on our way to Dragon Phoenix Wine Consulting. Located on a high floor of a nondescript building, Dragon Phoenix is one of the places where Beijing consumers and aspiring wine professionals can enroll in world-renowned wine education programs of the British Wine and Spirit Education Trust, or WSET. Over the last decade, the organization has seen an astonishing surge in interest from Chinese wine enthusiasts. China has become its second-largest market (after the UK), and by far the fastest-growing one. [15]

Dragon Phoenix was founded in 2006 by British-Chinese expert Fongyee Walker and her husband, poet and literature professor Edward Rag. Both were on the Cambridge University wine-tasting team (yes, there is such a thing), and eventually Fongyee decided her study of classical Chinese literature might not lead to a lucrative career. Instead, they moved to Beijing and got into wine consulting and education, and Edward also taught English literature (as well as the first-ever wine course) at Tsinghua University. Armed with their varsity wine experience, they worked their way up to the highest level of WSET (level 4, known as the diploma) and built a strong local team. Not only are they both fluent in Mandarin (and thus can teach in both languages), but in 2016, Fongyee became one of the world's 340 masters of wine, which requires years of study, grueling exams and blind tastings, and a final research project. After all that, you get to put "MW" after your name and become one of the world's wine Jedi. If anyone wants to study for the WSET level 4 in Mainland China, Dragon Phoenix is (at the time we are writing this, at least) the only place certified to do so by the mother ship.

WSET has such a strong global brand that it's hard to imagine a local Chinese program knocking it off the wine education pedestal. But still, we also wanted to see what a more homegrown, not foreign-owned, wine education business looked like.

We found such a place a couple of years later, during our month spent on a university exchange program in the beautiful city of Fuzhou, the capital of Fujian Province. Our research assistant, Dora, then a graduate student in English-Mandarin interpretation, got us an appointment at a little wine shop aptly named 101 Wine. The enthusiastic owner, Mr. Huang, used to sell hotel equipment in Shanghai. He had no professional wine background, but the love of drinking it led him to a new sales job at one of China's wine giants, Great Wall. A year later, he went on to sell wine on his own. Eventually, he enrolled in a formal wine course to improve his knowledge and tasting chops, starting up the path to becoming a wine educator. That alone was a remarkable success, given that Mr. Huang's family couldn't afford for him to complete high school. But there is more to 101 Wine.

The wine shop came first, then the school, and Mr. Huang had once thought of starting his own winery. But one evening, as he was watching a Korean TV show for foodies, a better idea popped up: a restaurant. "How did you choose Italian?" we asked. Not yet set on a clear direction, he'd posted an ad to recruit a chef on an internet job board. His favorite candidate happened to be an Italian food expert. That's how, just a few months before our first visit, 101 Wine expanded into an Italian restaurant.

Mr. Huang's first passion is traveling. And it is the love of travel that drives his passion for wine and food. Once, he caught an episode of CCTV's (China Central Television) popular show *A Bite of China*, about the village of Nuodeng, in Yunnan Province, where locals carry on a centuries-old tradition of harvesting salt and using it for food preservation. And with that salt, they make cured ham from local free-range pigs.[16] It didn't take long for Mr. Huang to get on a plane, visit the village, spend time with locals, and come back with a ham he serves as a delicacy in the restaurant. It's easy to assume that world-famous European versions of Jamón ibérico and Prosciutto di Parma must be the only, first, and best version of the product. But of course food preservation and alcoholic fermentation techniques were independently invented by indigenous communities around the world.

Mr. Huang doesn't teach WSET courses. But take the first three letters, reverse them, and you get China's own homegrown program: ESW, Ease Scent Wine Education. Like WSET, ESW provides teacher training and certification and licenses independent providers to teach its programs. Mr. Huang is a licensed ESW educator. ESW was founded in 2004, but it didn't start as a wine training program. It was the China distributor for a classic wine education tool: Le Nez du Vin (The scent of

Mr. Huang carving ham at 101 Wine.

wine). If you don't know what it is, you might remember a scene from the movie *French Kiss* when French-accented Kevin Kline and Meg Ryan play with a box of little bottles filled with flowers and herbs designed to fine-tune your nose on the complex aromas of wine. The commercial version is known as Le Nez du Vin, a kit of vials filled with aroma essences. That's hours of party fun, of course, but also a classic tool in wine education, more convenient than crushing fresh raspberries in cheap wine samples (though that leads to hours of fun too). With the increasing popularity of wine education in China, you can see why the makers of Le Nez du Vin cared about having a foot in the country.

Beyond distributing Le Nez du Vin, ESW's niche was to offer WSET-like courses entirely in Chinese. Although WSET now offers its introductory, intermediate, and advanced levels in Mandarin, not so long ago only English-speaking Chinese wine enthusiasts could enroll. WSET was not even in China yet when ESW launched its first beginner's course in March 2005. Four years later, the intermediate level was ready, and by 2011, an advanced level was finally available. Mandarin speakers could finally enjoy WSET-like courses tailored to their needs. In fact, when WSET started in China in 2006, ESW was the country's first certified provider. ESW now not only offers WSET introductory to advanced programs, but also is certified to teach for the International Sommelier Alliance and has education cum promotion partnerships with the official wine associations of Bordeaux, Germany, and Napa Valley, among others.

The introductory ESW course, level 1, is modeled after its WSET equivalent. Sure, ESW may not have the global aura that wine professionals seek to put on their resumes, but it is much cheaper: 880 yuan versus 1,480 for the British course. And there's even a chapter on Chinese wine, something you wouldn't even hear about until very late in your WSET studies (we hear they are working on something, but for now even the level 3 textbook doesn't mention it). It's understandable, of course. We get that Seattleites or Londoners seeking a WSET certificate to boost their career don't desperately need to know about the fine wines of Ningxia. But we love that Chinese wine newbies can get a course that not only is in their own language but also acknowledges local wines.

Some people take the class for professional reasons. But most of Mr. Huang's students, often white-collar workers in their twenties or thirties, come simply because they are getting interested in wine. And if they want to explore the wine regions they learned about, all they need to do is look around the shop. Like many in the trade, Mr. Huang has seen the market shift from gifts and status concerns to actual taste and a search for value. His most popular wines, he said, are those priced at 100 yuan or less. His enthusiasm for wine, food, and the people behind the products makes 101 Wine a place for locals to learn about wine, whether they take ESW courses or just come with friends for a meal. That's the kind of place where, we hope, more good Chinese wines can find their way. But there's a long way to go. While there are now many outstanding producers, their wines are often expensive compared to similar-quality imports. Mr. Huang knows a lot of Chinese winemakers, but for now, he only carries one Chinese wine he found to be the best value during his latest tour of Ningxia.

* * *

Like Mr. Huang, Yanzhi's success came from selling imported wine to the growing pool of Chinese wine enthusiasts. He'd been very good at marketing wines of the world, and his Bordeaux degree helped make him an authority in the business. But at heart, he was still a winemaker, and a dream brewed in his mind for many years: making his own wine in China.

Like many over the past decade, he set his eyes on Ningxia, which is what brought him to Kanaan winery that day we first met. He had recently gotten a lease on newly available land at the foot of Helan Mountain to plant vines. A year after our first conversation over a bottle of Bordeaux white wine in his Beijing office, we reconnected with him on WeChat, China's ubiquitous social media platform, hoping he remembered us. By the way, if you plan to keep in touch with friends or business contacts in China, don't put too much hope in your email. Just download WeChat. It only took an hour for Yanzhi to respond: "I'll be delighted to show you our vineyard and to tell you about our little adventure." We'll tell you more about Yanzhi's Ningxia wine adventure later in this book. But for now, let us take you on a wine summer vacation on the east coast, where Chinese wine, and wine tourism, began.

2

SEA, SAND, AND SHANDONG

It was serendipitous that we ended up on the beautiful coast of Shandong, with its sandy beaches and romantic restaurants, on Qixi, the Chinese version of Valentine's Day. We were traveling with our colleague, Jeff, an adventurous traveler with enough Chinese to get into trouble. This is even more so since Jeff's then wife had stayed in Seattle and, no matter how much he emphasized he was married, he seemed to get quite a bit of attention. That he found himself declining offers at 4:00 a.m. in the Qixi-themed nightclub was to be expected. The unsolicited calls to his hotel room from would-be escorts took him by surprise. We probably also got such calls, but since we didn't understand them, we assumed a wrong number. For us, the city of Yantai was brimming with kitsch and romance. Our hotel bathroom was adorned with stickers with cute animals and hearts. And on the bed, we found towels folded into heart-shaped kissing swans.

We made the mistake of overfilling our schedule and requesting a meeting with renowned Chinese wine journalist Jim Sun just as he returned from a business trip on the erstwhile romantic evening. Of course, he and his wife were incredibly gracious as he led us through a tasting to showcase some of China's best wine regions. It was only later that we considered the couple may have better things to do than a 7:00 p.m. meeting with economists.

His shop was in the perfect romantic space, near Yantai's "World Wine Walk." The pedestrian path connects the road to the crowded sunny beach, and it's lined with facades of shops named after world wine regions. A young man with a burgundy-colored shirt and black pants held his fiancée, whose red dress was a great match for the red circle–shaped sign of a shop referencing wines of . . . Niagara. We never figured out why the gate that led to it was behind a giant yellow rubber duck, but this, too, was photo-worthy. In any case, Yantai is a must-see capital for a wine tourism enthusiast in China.

What makes the city so special? It turns out that this is where Chinese wine began, longer ago than you might think, in the late nineteenth century. When we prepared for our first China trip, we jumped straight to the index of our brand-new 2013 *Lonely Planet China* and searched for the word "wine." Of course, this was no California or France travel guide. But we were pleased to find at least one mystery wine destination: the Changyu Wine Culture Museum, in Yantai. Back when we began our China wine adventure, that was the only place the Lonely Planet sent English-speaking tourists looking for wine in the country.

Changyu was the first winery, and to commemorate this, in 1992, they built the Changyu Wine Culture Museum. Only a short walk from the

Yantai's World Wine Walk: A great place for wedding pictures.

waterfront, conveniently located near other top sights, bars, and restaurants, the museum attracts large groups of tourists who are happy to take the guided tour and hear the story. Since then, a booming wine industry has developed in the province, including many wineries designed as attention-grabbing tourist attractions.

When Changyu opened the first modern winery in China, founder Zhang Bishi had help from an Austrian vice consul and winemaker, Baron Max von Babo.[1] It is one of the first names you learn on the tour, but it could have been someone else. When the company was founded in the early 1890s, the first foreign consultant, an Englishman who had signed a twenty-year contract, fell ill before he was due to arrive and died of a toothache gone wrong. The Dutch winemaker who followed him turned out not to be qualified. Von Babo got the job, and the rest is history.[2] "Babo" might ring a bell for dedicated Austrian wine enthusiasts. It is another name for KMW, the standard measurement of grape ripeness still used today to classify Austrian wines. KMW was invented by Max's father, August Wilhelm Freiherr von Babo, an important figure of Austrian viticulture and enology.

The place was designed to promote Changyu's brand, of course, which is well known thanks to its overwhelming market share and supermarket shelf space. But there is a clear effort to teach visitors about wine and viticulture, with details on each aspect of production. Armed with knowledge from the museum, tourists can head out of the city toward Chateau Changyu Castel, a joint venture with the Castel wine group from Bordeaux. It's close to a popular water park, and the new construction we saw in 2013 gave a sense of ever-expanding options. There is a museum component here too, but this one is a ginormous working winery. Unlike our Beijing Changyu trip, there were large buses of tour groups, exiting en masse, walking through the vineyard ("Don't Pick!" one sign said). They took the guided tour of the winery, observing the large stainless-steel tanks and taking pictures of the long rows of oak barrels, or in front of the display riddling station for sparkling wine bottles. On the way, our taxi driver told us he didn't drink wine, but he recited with pride how the winery got started in 1892 by Zhang Bishi. We invited him along, and he enthusiastically took even more pictures than we did.

The winery tour included a tasting in the bar with views over the vineyard, as well as a percussion set, two foosball tables, and coin-operated barrel dispensers. Families seemed to have fun with the tasting, studiously following their guide's instructions. But tastings weren't presented as the highlight of the tours. At the museum, the tasting was in the underground cellar, with prefilled glasses lined up and covered with plastic wrap, leaving the white wine samples awkwardly warm. Unlike in Napa, no one came here hoping to get tipsy. As one Chinese expert told us when we asked about these tours, if the tasting is deemphasized, it's probably not the best part. We knew that Changyu wine had won international awards, so why did they serve underwhelming wines to visitors? These museums did a good job promoting wine culture in beautiful spaces, but the wines themselves seemed to be extras on the set rather than main characters. Three years later though, on a return visit to the museum, the wines on the tour were good. Did this reflect a renewed focus on wine quality, or did we show up on a good day? Time will tell.

Changyu and wine street are just the beginning of a wine tourist route along the coast. We drove north to see where thousands of families plan their beach vacations, just a short hop from Beijing, Shanghai, and Seoul. Our hotel lobby was filled with an all-ages crowd, geared up with matching hats. The group was among two million visitors hoping to see a magical mirage at the Penglai Pavilion, one of the four great towers of China. Add glorious beaches, an ocean aquarium with dolphin shows, fresh seafood, and nightlife opportunities, and you can see why investors see wine tourism dollar signs in the making.

* * *

Eyes hidden under his red and white cap, standing still at the end of what could be his final putt, Todd Baek watched the ball roll on the green of the eighteenth hole. Done! The crowd roared as he looked up and waved at them. Confirming a five-shot lead, the six-foot-one former San Diego State collegiate player had just captured his first title since turning pro. As he held a long kiss with the glass trophy, the fact that the setting for this major career milestone was a Chinese winery was probably not too high on his mind. Baek's breakthrough title was on the PGA Tour China Series, at Chateau Junding Winery and Resort, a half-hour drive from the Penglai Pavilion. The PGA news story doesn't say whether he went wine tasting to celebrate.[3]

Overlooking a large reservoir, Junding's immaculate gardens and vineyards provide a green background to the buildings' California mission-style architecture and comprehensive resort. "We could have stayed here," we joked in a whisper. "The beds are probably way softer!" Junding guests could swim, get a massage, eat Chinese and Western food, play tennis, ride horses, and learn to play golf on a course nice enough to host a PGA tournament. Mind you, we study economic development. We met in an elevator in Bangladesh, where we took rickshaws on our first dates and visited women who borrowed microloans to sell handicrafts. During Cynthia's fieldwork in Senegal, we had a thin mattress on the tile floor, but not a bed. So, this new field of research—well, it took some getting used to.

When we visited a few years ago, Chateau Junding's main owner was COFCO, China's state-owned food-processing giant. The Junding experience included an educational winery tour, which we appreciated for its promotion of wine culture. In the Oak Education Room, we smelled different kinds of oak chips and learned about how barrels are made. We took notes and examined corks in the Cork Room. Then, we tried to hide our wincing grimace at the price list in the tasting bar. To be fair, the thirty to ninety yuan (five to fifteen dollars) per tasting looked like a bargain compared to the bottle prices. The most affordable Junding wine sold for three hundred yuan (fifty dollars).

One bottle price tag was especially memorable: 27,998 yuan, over four thousand dollars. Bring your selfie stick to show your Facebook friends you were standing next to this one. Apparently, that's a very special batch of only five thousand bottles to celebrate the founding of the winery. To get a sense of just how special that might be, blogger Jim Boyce suggested things you might enjoy for the same price. "Two round-trip economy class tickets from Beijing to Paris for RMB14,000, with the flight arriving early afternoon and leaving early the next afternoon, thus leaving me and a friend a full day and night and RMB14,000 to spend on food and drink. Or one round-trip business class ticket—requires stop in Moscow, but who cares—and RMB10,000 of spending money."[4]

We were glad to taste a handful of Junding wines at the bar without having to sell our car. But we got the message. They had glass bottles imported from France, most wine was aged in expensive new oak barrels, and they hired the world's most famous (and expensive?) wine consultant, Michel Rolland. And all that accounted for just a fraction of the final price tag. Junding didn't make wine for the rest of us. Here at Junding, the point was to feel like a VIP and imagine yourself among the photo gallery of famous "high-end members." Start sorting out who your truly special friends are. We'll let you speculate on what else you could do for the 150,000 yuan (more than twenty-two thousand dollars) joining fee.

Although the wines we tasted were good, our visit at Junding matched a prevailing stereotype of wine in China that we had reason to believe was on its way out. It was status but not taste, we'd heard, expensive gifts to be appreciated for what they represent but not necessarily for the taste. As one Junding salesman had put it in 2008, "China has no lack of rich people . . . , but these people don't know how to spend their money. Here, we are showing them how."[5] Indeed. But was this a sustainable business strategy? Apparently not. In 2016, COFCO sold its controlling 55 percent stake to its partner, Shandong Longhua Investment group, for, wait for it, one yuan. That's fifteen cents. It sounds like a great deal, until you realize that the new owner also assumed all debts in the tens of millions of dollars. More surprising, recently, the whole place was sold again to a new owner, for one dollar. Give them a call to see if they're looking for new investors, but beware. It turns out that authorities had banned new golf courses in 2004, so it seems that Junding Golf Club was in a regulatory gray area to begin with. Meanwhile, with brand-new wealth, tourism, and pressure to achieve economic growth targets, the number of courses exploded after the ban. But in recent years, President Xi's crackdown on lavish expenses in the government appears to have put an end to that.[6] We're not sure what it means for the Junding golf course.

Financiers played an important role in Shandong's wine expansion from the start. In fact, Zhang Bishi, Changyu's founder, is sometimes called East Asia's Rockefeller. We traveled up the coast to see the project of another wealthy investor, this time with an entertaining British twist.

* * *

"Chris Ruffle speaks. Woman astonished!" Our young tour guide in capri pants seemed to remember the scene quite vividly, still awed by his boss's Chinese-language skills. Our friend Jeff, an avid Chinese learner himself, was getting a bit jealous. Between bites of pizza and sips of wine, he had to ask, "Did he learn Chinese online?"

Well, no. Mr. Ruffle is British and studied Chinese at Oxford in the 1970s, back when there were only four students in the program. He ended up doing quite well in China, enough that in the 1990s, he bought and renovated a crumbling castle in Scotland. Today, his day job is to run Open Door Investment Management, a company he founded in Shanghai.

When he started Treaty Port Vineyards (the Scottish Castle) in a small village near Penglai, his wine background included having drunk wine previously. Now, the unusual castle is on Trip Advisor as one of the best B&Bs in Penglai.

It was hard to believe we were nearing a winery, much less a castle, as our taxi made its way through the village of Mulangou after getting off the main road. But one more turn and, voilà, the Scottish flag flapping at the top of the castle waved at us. Ruffle's wine journey started in 2004 when a French winemaker told him about a "lovely valley by a lake," near Penglai. A few months later, the project was underway, helped by local officials' drive to attract foreign investors. While close to popular tourist highlights, Mulangou was still a relatively poor and quiet village.

If done well, twenty hectares of grapevines and a winery could bring opportunity for local farmers, but unlike a factory, Ruffle claims, it can be done in a way that protects and values the environment. When he first saw the village back in 2004, the mud road was such that it only took one big rain to turn it into a vehicle trap. There were neither streetlamps nor any garbage collection.[7] As part of the deal, the government invested in roads, water, and electricity, and helped coordinate long-term leases with many farmers to assemble a vineyard from a patchwork of individual plots. By 2013 when we visited, roads were paved, a handful of bilingual street signs in front of a cute outdoor gym pointed to local highlights (including the "Scotland Chateau"), and streetlights were powered by solar panels.

It was all very nice on paper, with the best-laid plans and a supportive local government. Armed with his long experience doing business in China, Ruffle spent much time building relationships, which involves a fair amount of eating and drinking. He must have been very excited as the first harvest approached. But it all went downhill quickly. Rot in the vineyard plagued the first harvest. To make things worse, the consultant winemaker chose this convenient time to quit after being denied a raise. The fermentation tanks, which had been bought locally to avoid the hassle of importing, turned out to be poorly made. And some crucial imported equipment (including a press and a destemmer) arrived over three months late, in November. Sigh.

Despite all that, wine did happen, although not every year. Rain flooded the vineyard so badly in 2010 that it looked like the Amazon. But during our lunch in the library, surrounded by Ruffle's book collection,

Scottish castle in Mulangou.

we tasted a refreshing white blend of Muscat and Chardonnay, a nice red blend of Syrah, Grenache, and Cabernet Sauvignon, and the Treaty Port—Port fortified with the house brandy. For dinner, the lovely 2011 Merlot further fed our hopes for the castle's future.

That night, we sat in the dark under the covered spot on the castle's observation deck. A young woman braved the rain across the deck just to ask us what time we wanted breakfast served in the royal banquet room. Listening to the thunderstorm, overlooking rolling hills and the lake farther away, we felt like Hermione and Ron on a date at the top of Hogwarts. There was something surreal about spending the night in the Japanese room at the Scottish Castle in a small Chinese village.

Overall, our first Shandong wine trip left us with more questions than answers. We'd had some good and some not-so-good wine, as one would expect in an emerging wine country building its game. But the astonishing pace of construction of wine tourism amenities, which moved faster than the wine itself, felt unique. In other parts of the world, wine tourism can be boring for people who don't like wine. But here in Shandong, wine tourism seemed made to please regardless of one's taste for the drink. Was this a huge risk, or was it all very innovative? Make people step off the beach for an afternoon and come for the lavish castle selfies, and maybe some will stay for the wine. Between French, Scottish, California mission, and more traditional Chinese architecture, there seemed to be a different kind of kitsch wine attraction for every taste and budget. Photo opportunities waited at every turn. And as we'll show you next, there was much more underway in Shandong.

* * *

Four years after our first Shandong extravaganza, Pierre was back to Penglai on a solo mission to attend the Gourmand Awards, an international cookbook and wine book competition organized by Frenchman Edouard Cointreau (of the namesake French liquor family). Pierre was there to represent our friend Mike Veseth who had won a prize for his latest book. Chris Ruffle was there, too, receiving a prize for his own book, *A Decent Bottle of Wine in China*, a gripping and hilarious diary of his adventures with the winery. He'd brought with him liquid evidence of the

Chinese-style architecture on the Shandong wine trail.

book's cheerful conclusion to pair with the presentation: a few bottles for the audience to taste, celebrating his first truly successful vintage, 2014. Since our visit to Mulangou, new neighbors had moved in and wine tourism was about to get bigger in the village, for better or for worse. In fact, one of the new neighbors, a Frenchman, stood in the room during Ruffle's presentation, right after offering his own sales pitch and sharing his trial "Avant Premiere" Chardonnay. And the next day, he acted as the wine tour bus guide for a group of Gourmand attendees.

After an hour on smooth Penglai highways, everyone on the bus noticed the abrupt change as the ride got bumpy. We could all see that pavement would resume a bit further away, but getting to it seemed impossible. Several guests, perhaps anxious that the bus would tip over from maneuvering around the construction mess on this unfinished portion of the road, got off to wait outside. Thanks to the skilled driver, who could move the vehicle around better than we can parallel park our two-door Toyota Yaris, a few minutes later, we were finally in Mulangou. It had been four years since our first visit, and all we could think was . . . wow! The simple road from our pictures had become two comfortably large lanes with modern pavement. A beautiful stone wall and pretty flowers separated the new road from the rows of grapevines inspired by Burgundy. The tour guide of the day, Pascal Durand, an emeritus wine professor at the University of Burgundy, had advised the authorities on landscaping. At the beginning, the government wanted to destroy everything and make it all modern, but Durand and his team said, "No, no, no!"

Durand is a winemaker, but that's only one of his hats here, where he manages an intriguing winery retreat project. Once completed, Ruffle would have a new neighbor, with modern architectural plans announced on the billboard in front of a construction site. "Runaway Cow is not just a winery but a concept," Durand explained, describing the twenty-guest-room escape for "runaways" from urban life. A related enterprise, Runaway Cow's bistro in Shanghai, sources much of its produce from the group's own farm in Huzhou, one of China's famous silk towns, where another winery retreat was in the works. A Michelin-starred chef had already been prehired for the Mulangou winery's restaurant, Durand explained, and the kitchen will draw from the on-site organic farm. To make things fun for the whole family, kids will be able to pet and milk goats, not far from those millions of Penglai tourists looking for the next big thing in "agritainment."

Durand arranged lunch in the village so that the Gourmand group could experience local food. "A pig was killed for us yesterday. I've been here for two years and I've never been sick," Durand announced, clearly speaking to the foreigners who might be wary of local food and continuing to promote the farm-to-table message of soon-to-be Runaway Cow Winery Retreat. Pierre had expected a small family restaurant like the one where Scottish Castle manager Emma had taken us to dinner the first time. But in front of a small pond we recognized from our old pictures, all cleaned up and decorated, stood something we didn't expect: a Tourist Service Center. Three sentences in large red font on one of the outside walls remind visitors of the importance of promoting the strength and beauty of Chinese agriculture and the prosperity of its farmers. Seeing the pace of change in Mulangou was fascinating enough. But Durand had another tour planned the next day.

* * *

Welcome to Chateau Charm, one of Shandong's latest wineries to get in the game. Walking through the gate, we were greeted by two guards holding the salute. "Enjoy yourselves!" said our young host, a wine graduate from a university near Xi'an, as she opened the curtains to reveal the view. Around the modern, two-story building, tables on the deck allow visitors to sit by the pond and admire the rolling hills. And in the middle of the welcome area sits a device Cynthia insists we must find everywhere we can: an enomatic machine, a fancy wine-on-tap device that preserves open bottles under inert gas so you can buy one tasting pour at a time.

It's not fair to the owners' ambition to suggest the place is just "a winery." Sure, the lunch and tour were at one winery (Chateau Charm). But the project is much bigger than that. Our eyes darted from one site to the next, trying to keep up with the guide. It's a winery! No, it's a valley! It's a . . . cluster! Welcome to the Pula Valley Wine Cluster! In economics speak, a cluster is when a group of firms and related businesses are located near each other. They benefit from economies of scale because there is enough action to support nearby suppliers and to attract customers. In most of the world, wine clusters happen over time. First a winery opens here, then another one there, and so on. Years pass, and often with a mix of enthusiasm and resistance from local authorities and residents, you have a full-fledged wine route, complete with hotels and restaurants connecting the dots between winemakers. Back when Robert Mondavi and other Napa pioneers posed for a picture in front of a sign that said "WELCOME to this world-famous wine growing region, Napa Valley," the "world-famous" part was decidedly overstated. Napa looked nothing like the wine tourism hub it is today. Sometimes, the opposition wins, as when California's Santa Rosa residents quickly said "no, thanks" to the noise, traffic, and busloads of fans predicted at a winery owned by Food Network star Guy Fieri. So, it takes time.

But who has time to waste these days? Instead of just building Chateau Charm and waiting to connect with future neighbors, why not build the entire neighborhood yourself? You can build your own wine cluster and even call it your own little wine region. First, get a hold of the land and plant vines. Then, build the tour-bus-friendly wine roads, and landscape with cherry trees. Next, make sure one showcase winery is ready to go (Chateau Charm), so wine can start to flow, like the Pula Valley 2014 Italian Riesling, which suggests the potential of the whole valley, not just one chateau.

Armed with this, and a competent kitchen staff, you can start finding wealthy people looking for fun things to do with their money. Investors can commit a stake in the valley and get wine with their own label on it, which is nothing new in wine promotion, of course. California lovers who are flush with cash can join the exclusive Napa Reserve Club for just $150,000, participating in the winemaking if they wish. With that investment comes the privilege of buying a specified quantity of estate bottles for the supposed bargain price of seventy-five dollars. Pula Valley looks a bit like this but takes the game further. You don't just join a country club with some right to get your hands dirty in the cellar. You can buy your own chateau blueprint, have it built, and do everything yourself—or better, hire a consultant winemaker to make wine for you.

There's been interest, as evidenced by the carved wooden road signs pointing the way to a handful of wineries, most still construction sites for now. Within a few years, if all goes according to plan, the Pula Valley is supposed to have not five, not six, but *one hundred* wineries. This is another example of what we were talking about earlier: build wine tourism amenities first, then make wine and let people come. And importantly, be sure to make the wine tourism fun for everybody, especially those who don't drink wine. At Chateau Charm, guests can already pick cherries in the orchard.

Meanwhile, the big are getting bigger. Near its Castel Chateau in Yantai, Changyu opened what is perhaps its most outlandish project to date. It cost nine hundred million dollars, and it's called the City of Wine. The wine theme park has several chateaux, including one making brandy, a "grape and wine research institute," and a "grape planting demonstration park," which, Changyu hopes, will promote not just their brand but also wine culture in Asia, and even support "the global wine industry for useful exploration in industrial cluster." Well, nothing like building your own cluster to help others explore clusters. That's how fast things are moving here. But there is serious competition further west. There are no beaches, but there's plenty of wine potential.

3

THE REVENGE OF THE XIXIA

The tumbling rubber noise, combined with the feeling that our taxi suddenly leaned to the left, didn't sound like good news. We were grateful for the good-natured driver we'd recruited on our first ride from the Ningxia airport in 2013. He'd never heard of Ningxia wine but was happy to help us find the one destination we had, Yuquan Manor. According to the guidebook published by a nice man we'd met on a train, Yuquan Manor was a gigantic, full-service resort. It seemed smart to start as tourists, somewhere that didn't require personal connections to find, though we did have to stop for directions. No matter. None of us was in a hurry, and we were happy to take in whatever we could learn. We smiled as the driver slowed for a few cows leisurely taking up the entire road. But, then, that ominous noise. We all got out to look pointlessly at the flat tire.

Would our first attempt to reach Ningxia wine country fail today? He put on the spare, but not trusting it to hold four passengers, he drove away to find a garage, leaving us with Jeff and our assistant Josephine on an isolated rural road in the middle of cornfields. Would he ever come back? Would he be able to find this random stretch of road again? At least the rain had stopped, and without an ounce of shade around, the cloud cover was nice. A kid hung precariously on the edge of her dad's bicycle seat, and they slowed a bit to stare, understandably incredulous about what these *laowai* (foreigners) were doing hanging out at the cornfield, in the middle of nowhere.

Fortunately, our driver came back, and soon the road signs brought reassurance. A tall green gate with red characters welcomed us to "Grape Town." The roads, all in excellent condition, were decorated with grape-vines. And thanks to the bottle-shaped signs indicating directions to various wineries, we made it to our sole destination of the day. We were relieved as we drove into Xixia King winery (apparently, it wasn't called Yuquan Manor anymore), but we did wonder about the total absence of visitors.

The old-fashioned European streetlamps on the road to the entrance were a bit tacky, but the beautiful architecture evoked the region's history. The *Xi* in *Xixia* means "west," so the name refers to the Western Xia dynasty, founded in 1038 by tribes who spoke Tibetan and practiced Buddhism. Somehow holding fragile peaceful relations with other groups, they ruled for two centuries. Their biggest mistake happened in 1219, when they declined Genghis Khan's request to support the Mongols' invasion of Islamic states in Central Asia. They even formed alliances against him, a relatively rare example of solidarity and resistance that we considered with reverence, despite the unhappy ending. Khan sought revenge, and by 1227, shortly after his death, the Mongols took control of Yinchuan and exterminated the Western Xia people almost entirely. The few Xixia tombs are all that's left today.

The province is hardly a tourism magnet, but it does have some popular highlights. The *Lonely Planet* guide recommended the Western Xia tombs, a hike at a national park on the Helan Mountain, caves with ten-thousand-year-old rock carvings, and a visit to the Western Film Studios, where many popular Chinese movies were shot. But according to "Why Go?" in the 2013 edition of *Lonely Planet*: "Best of all, the province sees few visitors, so when visiting these sites you feel as though you have the place to yourself." Great for the short lines and uncrowded photos, but probably not what the Ningxia government wanted to hear. Unlike Shandong, which is one of the richest provinces in China, the Ningxia Hui Autonomous Region remains one of the poorest. Not that Ningxia doesn't see any tourists, but there's much room to grow. The local government has embraced tourism as a tool for economic development, and wine is part of the equation. In contrast to Shandong, where wine amenities came to diversify offerings for an existing critical mass of tourists, the mission of Ningxia wine tourism was to attract more tourists to the region. Our first stop, Xixia King winery, was part of this effort.

According to the museum's exhibit on Western Xia history, the Xixia people enjoyed drinking. A Madame Tussaud–style scene depicted three Xixia men drinking from small cups. Several bottles of Xixia King wine added color to the table, although the alcoholic concoctions of the time were quite different from modern wine. Of course, we also took in the lessons about winemaking, grape varieties, and company history that reminded us of the Changyu museum. The building and local wine boom were brand new, but we learned that Xixia King winery was built in 1985 by the state-owned Ningxia Nongken Enterprise. Unsurprisingly, it was still the largest producer and vineyard owner in the region, with more than ten thousand hectares and plenty of shelf space at local supermarkets. Of course, the Nongken group was also leading the development of the "Grape Town," negotiating land leases with private wine investors who wanted to get in the game.

Three smartly dressed tour guides welcomed us to a tasting room with an impressive view of Helan Mountain through the large window. The wine was good and reminded us of what you'd expect from a ten-dollar Cabernet Sauvignon from Chile. We were suitably impressed, especially compared to our first museum tasting near Beijing. A guide asked if we wanted another glass and we nodded, assuming it was included with admission and she was trying to avoid waste. After all, there was nobody else in sight to finish it, and the open bottle wouldn't stay fresh for very long. After a lovely time, our host gave us the bill: six hundred yuan for the wine, about one hundred dollars. It turns out she was charging us for every pour and that bottle was more premium than we'd realized. We were lucky she hadn't opened one of the even more expensive wines we saw in the shop. We choked a bit while we laughed at ourselves, but the lesson learned in cross-cultural communication was well worth the adventure's price tag.

It was great to see the leading state-owned winery embrace Ningxia history, but we worried about the absence of customers and the bewilderingly high prices. We knew Chinese tourists wouldn't be dumb enough to drink wine without confirming that it was free or affordable. But still, would visitors interested in local history and culture be drawn to the wineries as well? Would local Muslim culture and food play a part in the new investments, despite the alcohol? Would kids and grandparents be interested in this kind of visit? Would any of this result in income for the local community, including Hui Muslims? Building so much, so quickly, seemed like a risky bet. In one of the poorest and most isolated regions, we wondered if we would soon find ourselves returning to a Ningxia wine ghost town. But the local government's strategy made sense. After all, wine tourism had transformed many regions of the world. Just look at the way wine transformed parts of arid eastern Washington, hardly a tourist magnet before the rise of Washington wine. So, authorities had good reason to think that the developing wine industry should involve broader investment in Ningxia. And perhaps it will help that the bottle that shook the wine world with a trophy in 2011 was from Ningxia. Somehow, a few days into our first trip, we had gotten the winemaker's phone number and we finally got up the nerve to call her.

* * *

Two days after our Xixia King visit, we had drunk the Ningxia Kool-Aid. True, our museums and supermarket tastings had brought more questions than answers, but we were seduced. We had attended the employee barbecue of a producer that made affordable wine we thought people would drink. And we had eaten the cheap local food that, along with the people, would bring us back to Ningxia every chance we got. Plus, we'd done our homework on the wines that had gained international acclaim. So, we were appropriately star-struck when we met the bubbly, famous deputy secretary general of the Ningxia Wine Industry Association and her bouncing little girl.

Appropriately nicknamed "Jing Aling," Zhang Jing greeted us for the first time with an affectionate smile, as if we were friends. As the owner of Helan Qingxue, she had made the Jiabeilan "Baby Feet," the winner of the 2011 Decanter Wine Awards that helped put Ningxia on the map. Her eyes twinkled when she told us about her daughter's footprints on the oak barrel, inspiring the name. She walked us through a Ningxia wine map and told us about the people betting on the future of Ningxia wine. For starters, the association of wineries and the bureau of local government stakeholders merged to form the International Federation of Vine and Wine of Helan Mountain's East Foothill.

There were plans for "many more wineries," Jing explained. And government support for those who showed promise. There would be land, loans, irrigation projects, invited winemakers, and a significant push to regulate quality, so that Ningxia wineries could develop a recognizable brand. Hopefully we would see recognized appellations, like in France, and consumers would start to recognize the varied terroirs of Ningxia. She talked about the potential for Syrah and other grapes in the North and hopes for more Riesling in the South. As for her own wines, she said with a wistful smile, "Every winemaker dreams of a great Pinot." We were still starstruck during the tasting, and we loved the wines, but it was hard to tell what they might mean for the rest of Ningxia.

We had to admit, the level of investment was already astounding. The previous year, in 2012, there were twenty wineries. By 2013, there were close to a hundred, many lining the budding G110 wine route that was as impressive as it was bewildering. But so many areas felt like an eerie hotel from a horror movie. The lights were on, but no one was home.

We knew that our assumptions were clouded by our experience in other countries. Economic development in China had challenged the assumptions of economists for years, after all. So, we were cautiously optimistic, and we thought there might just be something smart about all this infrastructure investment up front. It was amazing to see such a wine route already up and running given how young the local industry was. We were flabbergasted to discover how much more was under construction, with bottle-shaped signs pointing to wineries that didn't exist. We wondered what it would mean to develop so much wine tourism infrastructure before there was much in the way of actual wine and people drinking it.

This is decidedly not how wine routes emerged in the rest of the world. Whether it's New Zealand or California, the path was the same. First, a few pioneer wineries gained recognition with a few good scores in magazines, pointing attention to the region. With increased investment, a few more wineries popped up. And eventually, some sort of local wine association or local authority connected the dots, making it more convenient for tourists. Hotels, restaurants, and golf courses joined in the fun, and voilà, a new wine route was born.

The process is never as obvious as it seems. Sometimes, despite good recognition for the wines and a good number of producers, wine regions struggle to fully mature into wine tourism hubs. For example, Mike Veseth called the Yakima Valley "Washington State's invisible vineyard," because despite its large scale and the fact that it grows grapes for some of the state's most celebrated wines, it remains much less well known than you might think. Observers often blame the lack of tourist amenities. If only more people came to visit, maybe the Yakima Valley name would finally be in every wine lover's mind. The problem is that amenities aren't worth building until enough tourists come, but people won't visit until there are enough amenities. Veseth points out that many famous Yakima growers sell grapes to wineries in other parts of Washington, so there's no obvious place for the tasting rooms that inspire hotels and restaurants.[1] Wine tourism doesn't grow around grapes alone.

Ningxia wine authorities were eager to tackle this classic problem right away, so it wasn't surprising that the next few years of policy making matched what Zhang Jing was describing in 2013 while her daughter pulled on her capri pants and convinced us all to stop and snack on delicious watermelon.

The regulations were designed with equal commitment to wine quality and broader economic development. Investors seeking Ningxia government subsidies had to promise more than just wine. They needed a commitment to grow at least some of their own grapes and build a tasting room that could welcome enough guests. This is why Ningxia's first official ranking of the best wineries required amenities for tourists. They called it the Classification of Ningxia Wine, a nod to the famous ranking system in Bordeaux. In 1855, Napoleon III asked local wine merchants for a ranking to display next to the wines at the upcoming Exposition Universelle in Paris. The merchants ranked the wines based on the most objective criterion they could think of—their market prices. They made it clear that their five tiers, or "Growths," didn't necessarily represent a definitive ranking, but somehow, the 1855 Classification has not only held up but also influenced the global wine industry ever since.

And so it was that the 1855 Classification served as a model for Ningxia, as is evident from its name and its five Growths. As in Bordeaux, producers who made it on the list could show it off on their label. Some skeptics argued that it was far too early for Ningxia to establish a quality ranking when the industry was so new. They may have had a point, but the Ningxia Classification served a much larger purpose. It seemed to us to be much more about regulating local wine production early. Details included rules on vineyard plantings and yields and requirements that the wine be made and bottled at the estate and that wineries develop decent wine tourism facilities. Moreover, every two years, a panel of experts and consumers would evaluate wineries.[2] Only time will tell whether it worked, but we were optimistic about the effort to promote quality while betting on the economic development benefits of tourism.

Of course, smaller wineries felt the pressure. On top of fulfilling minimum scale requirements, building spaces for tourists was expensive and time-consuming. At Kanaan winery, where we started this book, Crazy Fang remembered one visit by government officials who were impatient that the building wasn't finished. Her wines had earned praise, but that wasn't enough. If only she could rob a bank to finish faster, she joked. And what if you simply didn't have the space? The emphasis on tourist amenities could lead to strange results. When the first Ningxia Classification came out, Silver Heights, a winery that many critics saw as one of the very best in China, was not on the list. What's a wine ranking without one of the best producers on it? They had the great wines, made by Bordeaux-trained winemaker Emma Gao and her Bordelais husband, Thierry Courtade (formerly of Chateau Calon Ségur). They had the great small producer story that wine enthusiasts love. But they really had nowhere to put up a chandelier. The little farm and garagiste operation where we met them was not the government's idea of the future of wine in Ningxia. Fortunately, Silver Heights was able to lease new land and build a bigger winery with more space, conveniently much closer to the rock carvings and the West Film Studio that Lonely Planet recommends.

Meanwhile, the Chinese wine giants, those big brands you are most likely to run into at any supermarket in Beijing, had moved in. We wondered if their long-established national fame would help attract wine tourists, and they didn't hesitate to build impressive facilities.

* * *

Our taxi knew where to go. No GPS needed, the driver assured. By 2015, Ningxia wine was well known, and we no longer got concerned looks when we announced our destinations. Driving south on the G110 along the ever-magnificent Helan Mountain after our last winery stop of the afternoon, he confidently turned left back in the direction of the city, Yinchuan. We were looking forward to our dinner at Chateau Yunmo, a winery owned by one of China's wine giants, Great Wall.

A year earlier, Mr. Ma, the general manager, and his son George, who loves to practice English, had kindly given us a tour of the winery. Surrounded by vineyards, the modern structure stood out. In the winery, we climbed over a labyrinth of bridges that allowed employees to move safely across the room from one massive stainless-steel tank to the next. Add to this the dark underground cellar with long rows of oak barrels, and we could tell it wasn't boutique wine territory. This place was set up to make *a lot* of wine. Great Wall is the wine division of state-owned megaconglomerate COFCO, with tens of thousands of people on the payroll. When European governments negotiate to increase their pork or milk exports to China, they can go through COFCO. The portfolio is so diverse you could almost plan a vacation exclusively around COFCO brands. Stay at the Beijing Waldorf Astoria, eat the cereal and milk, drink juice and wine, and spend entire days at their shopping malls.

Great Wall, with its memorable name and state-owned prowess, is often the only Chinese wine foreigners have tried, and not always with positive results. But Yunmo was one of the group's new flagship labels that could help change that. Served appropriately cold, the Italian Riesling and rosé of Cinsault were lovely. The pricier red, a Cabernet Franc, won a bronze medal at *Decanter* magazine's Asia Wine competition.

When we visited in 2014, construction workers moved wood and steel parts across the bare cement floor of what would become the dining room. Mr. Ma, hands on his waist, smiled as he browsed the horizon through the large windows. He knew the dinner view would be a hit. Between vineyards and the mountain, within walking distance, you could see two of the Western Xia Tombs, remnants from the ancient empire and a leading tourist attraction in Ningxia.

Fast-forward to the following summer, and here we were back on the road to dinner with Mr. Ma. But this time, the winery dining room was ready. Our day was so well organized. After a late afternoon appointment back with Zhang Jing at Helan Qingxue, Yunmo was just a ten-minute drive away.

Except that our taxi wasn't supposed to loop left back toward the city. An hour later, we were still on the road going in circles. Poor George, whom we'd called to the rescue, had to go back and forth on the phone between his dad, us, and our chauffeur to explain the way. Eventually, we made it, over two hours late. What we thought was a simple dinner with Mr. Ma, it turned out, involved several full tables, and we would sit at the one with executives. We were mortified and couldn't find enough words to apologize. We never found out what time dinner should really have started, but the VIP crew didn't seem to mind (or at least they hid it very well). Instead, everyone was all smiles and eager to chat. Dishes kept filling the lazy Susan, and Yunmo wine flowed generously.

We knew there would be more than a couple of "ganbei" toasts, the hallmark of the Chinese table that many foreign businesspeople dread. Literally "dry cup," *ganbei* means "bottoms up," and participants are very much expected to take it literally. Typically, a host comes over for some good wishes, clinks glasses, and shares in the toast. Knowing this, we had managed to convince the server to give us small tasting pours. But toward the end of the meal, as the fruit plates arrived, the middle-aged guy across the table caught on to Pierre's sneaky sobriety scheme. Looking at the server, he signaled and watched: "More. Nope, more. Some more. There!" Now, we both love wine, but our American friends are often incredulous at Pierre's penchant for gingerly sipping small quantities over a long meal. He tried to hide a small panic as he smiled. "Ganbei!" Yunmo's Italian Riesling is yummy, but that gulp from a big glass felt endless. It was a great night, even though we almost missed it.

A few years after our visit, Great Wall gave Yunmo a new name: Chateau Tianfu. The group seemed determined to improve quality not just in Ningxia but across their whole line from different regions. It seemed like a healthy response to growing competitive pressure from imports and increasingly demanding consumers. Meanwhile, another Chinese wine megabrand was using Ningxia as a flagship outpost for their wine quality, complete with an impressive chateau.

* * *

Barely past the front gate, we couldn't stop taking pictures. "Wait a moment!" said our tour guide, who went into the little office building. She was right. The pictures were even more impressive with the fountain jets turned on. It was only 9:30 in the morning, so the park's bells and whistles weren't on yet. "Dream of France," the brochure says. In an otherwise unremarkable neighborhood with refurbished roads and university campuses, Changyu's rendition of a Renaissance castle stands out. In the castle's entrance, paintings add a touch of color to the ceiling above the chandelier, and two cute little creatures cling to a Changyu bottle twice the size of a tall person. The first stop on the tour invites guests to watch a video presentation of the place, with an endearing foreigner who shows everyone all the things not to miss here, as he walks the cellar, sniffs wine with a passionate and intense facial expression, greets visitors, and dances with employees dressed in mascot costumes like at Disneyland. "Is he a foreigner?" our assistant Christy asked, her voice suggesting some awe for the young man's Mandarin skills. And as the film moved on to his savoring a steak at the winery restaurant, Christy turned to Pierre as if to check for authenticity: "Have you had this dish?"

As in Yantai, the museum teaches basic wine facts and Changyu history, but this one is much more interactive. To learn how wine might be good for your health, pick up the old rotary phone and listen to the story of the French Paradox, the fact that French people have relatively low rates of heart disease despite their famously rich, high-fat diets. If you think you might forget, the cartoon visual aid will seal the idea in your mind forever. On the right, an obese, presumably American man with a baseball cap and a "Go Team!" T-shirt is sitting on a bench eating unspecified takeout food straight out of the package, washing it down with cans of soda. On the left, a svelte Frenchman, complete with beret, curly mustache, and big nose, is eating his meal on a plate sitting at an outdoor café with a glass of wine. Get the idea? Wine is the secret, or at least wine is one popular explanation that has led to years of scientific research and effective wine promotion. When the TV program *60 Minutes* revealed this idea to millions of American viewers in 1991, red wine sales skyrocketed. On the Changyu cartoon, the wine-drinking Frenchman stood as a role model for Chinese consumers, who often cite health as a reason for choosing wine. We figured we should ignore the fact that the man was

Changyu Moser in Ningxia.

eating alone, cigarette in hand, having apparently consumed more than half of the bottle. It is a paradox, after all.

Moving on, the museum engaged visitors' senses. You could push buttons to release samples of classic wine aromas, trying to guess each one. Tourists played putting their hands on different parts of a giant tongue, marked with five areas, designed to light up and announce a different taste category: "Sour!" Now to the tip of the tongue: "Sweet!" And off to the back middle: "Bitter!" Pierre hurried to get a picture of the infamous tongue map. Scientists have discredited the concept, but you'll still find it in some wine books. To complete their sensory wine training, visitors studied the food and wine pairing chart. Bottles were organized by style, so that people could touch one and follow the path of lights to suggested foods. Later, selfies clicked as visitors took turns to memorialize themselves clinking glasses with the 3-D wall painting of Barack Obama. For kids who might be impatient by this point, the 3-D globe movie theater provided more all-ages wine education and Changyu marketing.

We thought the most fun part of Changyu Moser might be their weekly family day. Every weekend, eight to ten families can reserve a full day of DIY (do-it-yourself) fun with the kids. It starts early in the morning, in the winery's kitchen, where everybody makes their own breakfast and learns how to make bread. Depending on the season, you can pay a little extra to pick your own grapes. Then, it's time for a morning of fun with the game-filled winery tour, including a treasure hunt in the cellar and crafts projects for the whole family. Here's how it goes. First, visitors are invited to place a sticker label of their choosing on an empty bottle. Then, they walk over to the oak barrel, which has a tap to fill the bottle with the house brandy. Don't worry, it's all legal, as the kids can help to place the regulatory back label, specifying the 38% alcohol level. Finally, it's back to the worktable to hammer in a cork, and voilà, a nice gift for Mom and Dad.

We were astounded by the effectiveness of this kind of marketing but realized that they can't really try it in Napa Valley. First, the targeted advertising toward kids is illegal there. The Code of Advertising Standards laid out by the Wine Institute, an advocacy organization for California wine, forbids the use of anything "predominantly popular with children," such as cartoon characters, Santa Claus, and the Easter Bunny.[3] And since wineries can't make health claims in the United States, you probably won't learn about the French Paradox while touring wineries in Walla Walla. With no such rules in China, Changyu is free to make wine tourism fun for the whole family.

In many ways, Changyu's brand of wine tourism, mixing Disney, wine, and Renaissance castles, seems out of place. Some foreigners are surprised, asking why more Chinese wineries don't choose a traditional Chinese style. But for the most part, Chinese wine tourism isn't about foreigners. The goal is to build a brand with Chinese consumers, and the modern idea of wine in China is still heavily shaped by images of France. This is not exactly unheard of for an emerging wine region. Just look at Washington State in 1976, when Ste Michelle Vintners changed its name to Chateau Ste Michelle and built a French-style Chateau in Woodinville, near Seattle, now a hub of urban wine tourism. But not every Francophile has a penchant for European chateaux. Along the G110, you'll find more than a few Bordeaux-trained or Bordeaux-inspired winemakers looking for the best Ningxia terroir but not so much as a hint of European architecture.

* * *

Standing outside our hotel on a sunny Yinchuan morning in 2015, Pierre felt a tap on his shoulder. "Bonjour!" It was finally time for that vineyard visit we'd planned with Zhang Yanzhi, the Bordeaux-trained winemaker and importer you met in chapter 1. We couldn't wait to see his vineyard. We spoke French during the long ride to the site. As we passed the West Film Studio and turned right off the G110, we knew the vineyard was getting closer. As vineyards began to appear, the roads turned quieter and quieter, with almost no buildings in sight. Welcome to Jinshan, or gold mountain, the next larger-than-life wine project supported by the local government. We stood at the foot of the Helan Mountain on a bunch of rocks where Yanzhi and a few other investors took a seventy-year lease to build their own wineries. He called it Guanlan Vineyard because *guan* means "light" and is nicely followed by the second character in *Helan*.

During our first visit, the vines were still babies, and the first harvest was two years away. He preferred wood to steel for the poles supporting the grapevines' trellis. Not that it makes any functional difference, but he wanted to keep it all natural like the Bordeaux Grands Crus that had inspired him in college. Yanzhi had ambitious plans for a modern winery with stone walls, but the site, classified as "forest land," would take some time to get a construction permit through the authorities in Beijing. He spoke passionately about his focus on winemaking for Guanlan, but he also envisioned a small space for a restaurant, guest rooms, and, of course, a tasting room, which, as you know, pleases government officials.

The mountain views were stunning, but as we looked around to see nothing but a bunch of rocks and baby vines, it was hard to imagine. Who would come here to do this? Yanzhi liked the rocky soils, which reminded him of the left bank of Bordeaux. But more importantly, he believed in the government's push for wine in Ningxia, and like many other investors, he knew he would benefit from it. Jinshan felt like the middle of nowhere, but we were intrigued by its short drive from major tourist sites like the West Film Studio. We were just a bit off the existing wine route, and authorities were betting on Jinshan to be the next step. Guanlan Vineyard soon had more neighbors with baby vines. Yanzhi explained that a major strength of Ningxia for wine investors is that they're not alone. Investors came together building a diverse wine region with government support to secure land, build an irrigation system, and develop regional promotion.

Waiting for his first harvest, with the winery only drawn on paper, Yanzhi started his wine experiments by buying grapes from trusted farmers and leasing space at local wineries to make his first wine. Two years after our first visit, the grapes were finally coming along nicely. But authorities were still playing hard to get with the construction permit.

* * *

With close to a hundred registered wineries (and more underway) by 2016, the pace of construction and scale of Ningxia's wine tourism plans were baffling. But what about the history and culture and wicked barbecued lamb that make Ningxia so distinctive? Would successful wineries end up feeling like some region-wide gentrification, with big investors and beautiful buildings that make you forget the people of Ningxia? Would the wine we enjoyed ever be sold at prices that regular people could afford?

In 2016, we were back on the G110 (isn't it convenient?) on our way to Chateau Miqin, one of many wine destinations to open in the year after our first visit. Its production was relatively small, with only about eighty thousand bottles per year, mostly red, but also half bottles of off-dry rosé. Like Xixia King, Miqin's architecture is in the Western Xia style, and again, we wondered if this reference to local history would be able to do justice to the region's distinctive roots. The winery tour and museum were nice, but we had grown blasé about this sort of thing by now.

Then we saw the bottle prices: eighty-eight yuan (about twelve dollars) per bottle for a simple but pleasant Cabernet Sauvignon, and the flagship Cab went only up to 128 yuan per bottle. Compared to the high price tags of many good (and sometimes not-so-good) Chinese wines, Miqin offered remarkable value. The winery tour itself was standard: fermentation tanks, barrel rooms, a small exhibit with bottles, pictures of the winemakers, a text explaining wine and health, and more information on wine culture, with references as diverse as Napoleon, Marx, Van Gogh, and Tang Dynasty poet Li Bai. We could imagine regular people enjoying this visit and, equally important, paying for the wine, which was a big step from our first visits, but it was still just a winery—now, we feared, a dime a dozen.

Our host suggested we take a walk around the grounds, and that's when we understood what the place really was. Chateau Miqin was a small part of a much bigger project: a 167-hectare theme park devoted to Western Xia history and culture. And there was more to it than just text, pottery, and ceramics. We had arrived just before closing, so it was quiet,

Ancient battle reenactment at Miqin.

but a few ambitious parents and energetic kids wandered the grounds. It started with a sign for an organic poultry farm. Cynthia gets excited about food and cuteness in equal measure, so she cheerfully greeted the active, uncaged chickens while happily announcing her intention to eat them and looking for the associated restaurant.

We walked awhile before really getting a sense of the size of the place. Set around a little lake, with views of the mountains on the horizon, the park includes beautiful gardens, imperial buildings, and a traditional Western Xia village market street with all kinds of little shops and photo opportunities. In the village, a little stage features folk performances with martial artists, knife-throwers, and fire-eaters. But perhaps the most stunning part is the huge horse battle arena. On weekends at 11:30 and 4:30, muscular stuntmen, dressed as ancient warriors, spar with swords, spears, and shields to reenact legendary battles of the times, performing spectacular acrobatic feats on their horses. It was too late to see the battle, but we took pictures in the arena, placing our heads in cutout photos of ancient soldiers, and read about the cultural origins of various crafts. But Pierre longed to see the performance. Finally, in 2018, leaving Cynthia sick in the hotel, Pierre took the bus for one yuan and came home with a video of the ancient battle reenactment, complete with gory, bloody special effects to delight the children in the audience.

4

TAI DUO LE! TOO MANY!

On the eve of China's National Day, Hu Jintao was visiting a mushroom farm in Xiaogang, a poor, unassuming village in Anhui Province. Millions of viewers around the world had watched the general secretary launch China's first Summer Olympics three months earlier at Beijing's National Stadium. But for Chinese farmers, the Xiaogang visit was more significant. It was there that, in 1978, Yen Hongchang and seventeen of his neighbors decided to risk their lives by signing a secret document that would change China forever. Back then, farmwork was a collectivist, top-down affair. Farmers gave everything to the government and got paid the same—nowhere near enough—allotment of food rations, no matter what they produced. Why spend precious calories getting more out of the farm if you couldn't eat or sell it anyway?

The secret contract, hidden in the roof of Hongchang's house, gave each member responsibility over a specific plot of land.[1] They would fulfill their required crop delivery to the commune, but anything beyond that was theirs to keep. From the government's perspective, it all looked the same. But now, knowing they would enjoy the fruits of their labor, farmers grew way more. A great idea, except for one thing: the arrangement was completely illegal.

A year later, local party cadres discovered the scheme, and poor Hongchang was summoned to a heated meeting that must have felt like the road to execution. Fortunately for him, it was a time of deep political change for China, and it turned out that the officials were open to the idea. They just couldn't deny there was something to it, given the dramatic improvement of the team's performance. Officials allowed the villagers to experiment with the system, as long as it didn't spread. But spread it did. Its official offspring, the Household Responsibility System, became a cornerstone of Deng Xiaoping's rural reforms. Economists estimate that as much as 78 percent of the enormous improvement in agricultural productivity in China between 1978 and 1984 can be attributed to the incentives created by the new system.[2] Now, it is highly possible that this kind of undercover reform took place in more than one village. But today, the village of Xiaogang is known as the birthplace of an innovation that unleashed rural transformation and economic growth, a nerd magnet for history buffs who flock to its Memorial Hall of the All-Round Contract System.

What does an old secret document that transformed China's economy have to do with the struggles of today's winemakers as they try to grow good wine grapes? To find out, let's head to a large winery with beautiful tourist amenities near the city of Kunming, in Yunnan Province.

* * *

Ever since our arrival in Yunnan the day before, the city of Mile (*meeluh*) had been under a deluge of rain. We had landed at Kunming airport, an hour's drive away, and our shoes were soaked by the time we crossed the street from the terminal to the bus station. You can see why it's called "Spring City," where everything is beautiful and there are flowers year-round. On our way to Yunnan Hong, the local wine giant, it was still raining, and we were confused. We soon learned that summer is monsoon season, a tough lot for grape growers who like things sunny and dry.

Everything was so lush, green, and wet, it felt like a rainforest. We dreaded seeing vines with the waterlogged grapes and the too-comfortable home for insects, bacteria, and fungi that we imagined destroying the 2014 vintage. But we knew we must be missing something. This rain was obviously not unusual. Rickshaws and bicycles were outfitted with tarps, and people from all walks of life were going about their day. It was the second week of August. How could they possibly get ripe grapes to survive until September? In farming communities, people are usually happy to talk about the weather and the year's harvest, so we alleviated some of our ignorance before we got to the winery. No worries, our driver explained, the harvest was finished a week ago. Really? We stared out the window in disbelief and tried to hide our incredulity as we came up with neutral questions. What is the growing season like here? Well, for starters, this far south, it starts in February.

At the winery, we learned that rain evaporates very quickly, which helps with disease but doesn't overcome what is fundamentally a monsoon climate. We were used to Cabernet Sauvignon and Merlot, Bordeaux varieties that dominate the world market and Chinese wine production. But wine in Mile is made with local grapes like Rose Honey or French Wild. We love that these only-in-Yunnan grapes are cool and distinctive, but they're also disease-resistant and they ripen early (sometimes even in June), so they do well even if they can't stay on the vine as long as the winemakers would like.

Of course, it's complicated. Yunnan Hong makes about ten million bottles a year and has to guarantee that at least half of its volume is produced with contracted grapes from local farmers. When we asked Mr. Shan, the general manager, how many farmers they work with, even we, with our limited Mandarin, didn't need to wait for the translation to understand his answer: "Tai duo le!" Too many!

After all, the Household Responsibility System is designed to allow each family to use the land it has been allocated. No one is allowed to buy or sell it because, technically, it belongs to the village collectives. This system has kept agricultural land divided between countless tiny family plots. How do you work with so many different groups of people? How do you coordinate contracts, establish consistent viticulture practices, and negotiate prices? And how do you deal with the most blatant and ubiquitous clash of incentives: winemakers want small clusters of concentrated grapes with little water and tons of flavor, but they pay by the kilogram, which means farmers want big, heavy grapes.

When farmers show up at Yunnan Hong's door with their trucks to deliver the grapes after harvest, the result is an epic traffic jam that customers won't get near. Moreover, each transaction can take some time. You can't just weigh the grapes, multiply the number by the price per kilo, and say, "See you next year. Next, please!" For the planting company staff, the work starts during the growing season by going to the vineyards, tasting the grapes, and talking with farmers to make sure they follow instructions. Once the grapes arrive at the winery, the winemaking team inspects them and rejects those that don't meet the standard. This is where things get sticky.

Some quality indicators are easily observable. You can get sugar levels by squeezing a bit of grape juice into a refractometer, to check whether a sufficient level of alcohol would be reached after fermentation. You can also reward quality, as Yunnan Hong winemakers do by making it clear they'll pay more for Rose Honey grapes with higher brix (the standard measurement of sugar ripeness). And at a glance, they can check the general condition and color of the grapes: "Nope, sorry, not these green ones; our Rose Honey grapes need to be dark red, OK?" Some things are obvious, but at the end of the day, grape quality is subjective, meaning it's up for debate.

This problem is by no means unique to China. Famous wine-producing countries like Australia and Spain have long histories of relationships between farmers and wineries, and no lack of legal recourse. Yet disputes between wineries and independent grape growers are legend, and they've got mountains of research (and lawyers) trying to get a handle on it.[3] Even in Champagne, one of the most highly valued wine regions in the world, the whole business depends on a delicate balance between the interests of small growers who own most of the land and big Champagne houses that sell most of the wine. Sure, in established wine regions, growers have a lot of experience working with wineries. But there is still room for disagreement once the grapes are delivered and it's time to negotiate the final price. In 2011, the Napa Wine Symposium filled the house with a panel where lawyers acted out a skit, role-playing some of the ways grape contracts run amok, and they posted the whole thing on YouTube. Whether it's China, California, Australia, or France, these problems are a fact of life for wineries.

Of course, it's even harder in rural China, where most farming contracts are unwritten and difficult to enforce. Agribusinesses often interact with hundreds of small farmers, but how do they do it, and how much power do poor farmers have? In Mile, farmers can't really sell grapes to another winery as they might in Ningxia, but they can certainly grow other crops at similar prices. The aromatic Crystal variety is also popular as a table grape, which means farmers can just decide to grow them bigger and sell them as snacks. The key is specific arrangements that protect poor farmers and give everyone a reason to keep coming back. Farmers might need guaranteed minimum prices. If a company accepts the guarantee, they can also require farmers to make specific investments that are only useful if they stick with the contract.[4] For irreplaceable thirty-year-old vines, the winery has to pay farmers in advance to make sure they won't pull them.

Some growers are also employees of the winery, so they get priority over grape contracts. That makes perfect sense when you think about the need to enforce contracts privately. Working with people you trust, or who depend on you in some way, must make things easier. Now you see why economists talk about trust more than you might think. But remember, China is gigantic, and lush green Yunnan only has so much in common with the beautiful desert in Ningxia. To learn more about how Chinese wineries can work effectively in a seemingly impossible grape supply chain, there is no better next stop than one of the leading wineries in China.

* * *

"What do you think about this wine?" "What about the acidity?" These are the questions we had to answer a few times as Tao, one of Grace Vineyard's winemakers, walked us from one exciting barrel sample to the next. It doesn't matter how many times we tell our hosts that since we're political economists, they probably shouldn't trust us with technical comments on their wines. But they understand who we are, and they care anyway, and maybe to show their respect, they often write down every word of our clumsy tasting notes. We are consumers, after all, even "exporters" if you count our own basement.

Here in Shanxi Province, where Grace had gotten started almost twenty years earlier, it was only our second winery visit, so our experience with Chinese wine was limited. We fell in love with Grace from the very first sip, taken from a barrel of 2012 Marselan, a grape variety that was born from crossing Cabernet Sauvignon and Grenache in the Languedoc region of France a few decades ago. "It's a good blending grape because of its deep color," Tao said, but even he was impressed with the wine. It was so bright and lush, we weren't at all surprised when it was released three years later as a new single-varietal wine.

A couple of hours later, we walked down the path where the grapes came from. The view from the vineyard was stunning, overlooking green fields, including corn, as far as we could see. A Grace employee was doing his round in the vineyard to check for any pests, and a few farmers were working in the vines. As we walked down the vineyard, our wonderful and bubbly hostess, Bonnie, rushed under a net cover to pick some grapes for us to taste. It was Aglianico, an old grape variety notably grown in the South of Italy. We had just tasted the barrel sample that would rock one of our blind tastings two years later. Bonnie was smiling as she chewed on a grape and handed us our own. They were ripe enough for us, and birds, to enjoy (hence the net), but wine grapes get a lot sweeter than table grapes when they're ready to harvest.

Mr. Li, the field manager, took over answering most of our questions. You could see grape supply economics at work by looking down both sides of the path. On the right, we saw Grace's own vineyard on government-allocated land, where they can treat grapes exactly as they please with their own employees. Each of the vines and clusters looks the same, with the exception of those singled out for experimentation. Two of the plots stood out, equipped with a system of stakes and wires to support a plastic rain cover that could be deployed at the push of a button.

The left side was a very different story. Grace CEO, Judy Chan, had described this when we interviewed her over the phone, but we still had to do a double take when we saw onions and watermelons planted between the vines. Here again, individual farmers supplied most of the grapes. In Shanxi, Grace controlled a little over a hundred mu (about 6.7 hectares) of vineyard land, but the rest, more than three thousand mu, were hundreds of tiny plots operated by families. "Tai duo le," one might say! Too many! And yet, this had not prevented Grace from becoming one of the leaders for quality wine in the country.

In many places, poor producers don't have much choice but to take a bad deal, so we really wanted to know where wine grapes seemed to provide new opportunities. We asked Ma Huiqin, a grape scientist and Chinese wine expert, about relationships with farmers. "You definitely need support," she said. "Imagine you have a project. People will steal your equipment, your irrigation system, so you need local support. It's important to attend a village dinner, a local meeting. 'Investment' . . . it's not just about money, but respect, time. You have to show the farmers you understand their conditions."

When Grace imported their first grapevines from France in 1997, they taught local farmers how to plant them. Farmers were convinced by the promise of a higher income from grapes than alternative crops at the time. And to help seal the deal, Grace guaranteed grape purchases for the next ten years. The key to Grace's success in the vineyard was the relationships they established with their suppliers, several hundred families of farmers. It was a lot of work, sometimes frustrating, but that's what you have to do to get the grapes you want. We call it ethnographic winemaking because you must spend time in the community, thinking about what farmers need and what they care about.

We talked to Grace's first consultant winemaker, Frenchman Gérard Colin, who went on to spend two decades making Chinese wine in different regions. He loved farmers and vineyards, so it is no coincidence that he laughed off sideways glances and insisted on eating with farmers. One Chinese expert described him as "a local grandpa in the village," one of the only foreigners (and winemakers, for that matter) to move past being an outsider. He fondly remembered being in the vineyards every day, with three assistants, to give instructions to farmers. The team established a system of bonuses for following instructions and delivering better-quality grapes. After working with the same farmers for a while, Grace's winemaking team could sort them by quality and make decisions accordingly. They knew exactly whose grapes went into which bottles. This is essential when, like Grace, you produce a range of wines at different price points.

Now, it sounds very nice to have a system of bonuses to reward growers for picking later and for following instructions to ensure ripe and flavorful grapes. But you have to keep the relationships going as incentives inevitably shift. Beyond the grape price itself, working for a winery and constantly following specific instructions can feel a bit intrusive. Stressing the vines by irrigating less? Working to reduce yields? Pruning in specific ways based on some winemaker needs? Not all farmers complied with the same rigor. Guaranteeing purchases was useful to convince farmers to invest in wine grapes in the first place. But eventually, some growers were happy with the minimum price and didn't invest further. The contracts had to be redesigned to keep incentivizing higher quality. A lot of time was spent meeting with the local village cooperative that helped negotiate terms and prices. When farmers were unhappy, they could negotiate together for better prices or more favorable terms.

Grapes are just one of several crops families grow on their small farms. Grapes take precious space on their land. When Grace started, the income from wine grapes was higher than other crops, and the local government provided incentives to plant them. But more recently, subsidies for other crops went up, flipping the incentive the other way. Some growers, thanks to a few years of selling wine grapes, were able to save

Onions between the vines on a farmer-owned plot.

up, build a greenhouse, and move on to other crops. When that happens, you lose the fruits of years of efforts working with them. If growers don't have a guaranteed price, they'd better have a really good reason to stick with the winery. Enter the winter of 2013, with ice, hail, and freezing rain. What happens if the grapes aren't good enough? What if you lose whole vines? You might be better off pulling the vines and planting vegetables you know you can eat, particularly since new vines would take years to produce quality. Instead, Grace let them plant food crops between the vines, risking a bit of quality in the short term but protecting the farmers and the vines. That's good social responsibility, of course, but it's also an investment in future contract grapes.

* * *

During our first visits in 2013, we wanted to learn more from farmers, but we knew they would be easily threatened by an official interview. We stopped by a roadside umbrella in Shandong to buy some grapes and chat. The man we met was completely bald, with the unusually muscular agility and leathery light tan of a longtime farmer who nevertheless takes the time to protect his skin. He was old enough to have seen a different

China, with an attitude of someone who works hard but doesn't waste energy. Under his umbrella were a Chinese flag, large growlers of home-made fortified wine, and fresh peaches and pears.

Previously, he'd contracted with the state-owned wine giant Changyu. In the past, the prices for wine and table grapes were about the same. But in 2012, Changyu paid five yuan per kilo, when table grapes were going for more than twenty yuan. The winery didn't take any risk since they only entered contracts in the days before harvest, and once farmers had the vines, it was difficult to pull them. In 2013, he lost all of his wine and table grapes, so his entire income came from his own wine and other crops. We tried some of his fortified, sweet wine and liked it better than the Changyu museum tastings we'd had the week before.

His table grapes and sugar spend six months buried in traditional-style clay fermentation. It's more stable than dry wine and seems to please a variety of palates. We watched with fascination as two clean-cut, attractive businessmen pulled up in a Mercedes and negotiated the price of the jug of wine from 125 to 120 yuan, saving about seventy-five cents. For this farmer, the pressures come from everywhere, and the key is a diversified portfolio—more fruit, less risk. But if the buyers don't pay for quality, he obviously can't invest in it.

Not everyone was willing to pay a premium for quality grapes. Driving around wine country in August, year after year, we'd pass dozens of farmers selling table grapes by the roadside. For them, the price for big, heavy, watery table grapes was the same or higher than for wine grapes, even though they could grow far more on each vine. The farmers we spoke with told us that they'd had very little contact with winery buyers before harvest. In one area, growers brought their grapes to the winery at harvest after they had taken all the risk. At that point, they had to accept whatever they were offered. In another, the winery representative would visit two weeks before to set a price. Of course, many farmers depend on wage labor in addition to work on their family farms. During harvest in Ningxia, large winery-owned vineyards were filled with women picking by hand, making about ten dollars a day in 2018.[5] For political economists, farmers' working conditions are central to the story, so you can imagine how we struggled to keep a straight face whenever we heard complaints that farmers don't invest in quality because they "don't understand" or "need to be educated."

Meanwhile, everything we read told us that buying from hundreds of growers would be an insurmountable barrier to premium wine in China. Of course, we were always irritated by the attitude that challenges in the Chinese wine industry stem from some special, uniquely Chinese peculiarities. Westerners working in poor countries say this sort of thing all the time. In fact, you'll find the exact same grape supply story in another, now-famous wine-producing country.

* * *

"Cyn! Come here!"

Pierre screamed uncharacteristically from another room. The combination of excitement and urgency in our house almost always means something in the news—sometimes politics, usually wine. Next thing we knew, he was reading aloud from a history of one of the most remarkable wine successes in the New World: Argentina.

We often start our talks about Chinese wine with a few unattributed quotes:

> "The stuff the locals drink is invariably nasty aged in musty old wood if it's red; stale and lifeless if it's white."
>
> ". . . sometimes clumsy and thick"
>
> "Too many wines packaged in heavy bottles and carrying price tags of $30 or more deliver only modest fruit, lashed with overbearing oak."

The audience consistently giggles and, we presume, starts to worry a bit about the blind tasting of Chinese wines we have planned. There are usually plenty of wine geeks, and it's always an interesting moment when we reveal that these generalizations are not about China at all. This brief glimpse is how famous wine writers talked about Argentina in the late nineties and early 2000s.[6] And it turns out that one of the barriers to improvement was—wait for it—the local land regime and shaky grape contracts. When we read Ian Mount's thrilling history of wine in Argentina, *The Vineyard at the End of the World*, we found that we could easily be reading about China. Mount reminds us that "Argentina's vineyard land is owned by a quilt of small farmers spread over the Andean west."[7] And grape contracts were "The Waterloo" for those new to the business, he explains. To this day, most Argentine wineries buy a large portion of their grapes from many small growers. The top wines may be from wineries' own estates, but plenty of the mid-priced Malbec people have come to love in the United States comes from contract grapes. The international success of Argentine wine came not only thanks to wineries using their own estates but also from improved relationships between wineries and growers.

This has been central to wine improvement in China so far, but we also wonder whether expanding wealth from the wine industry will have any benefit for farmers, especially the poorest. Call us optimists, but we still hope the industry can head in this direction. It's not just Grace Vineyard that had to maintain good relationships with farmers. Among the wineries that have gotten attention from famous wine critics, many have built their first successes on bought-in fruit. In Ningxia, many award-winning wineries have made good wine in part with contract grapes. We'll meet some of them, and more, at the next stops of our journey. Of course, that doesn't mean that control over vineyards won't help farmers and bring Chinese wines to the next level. You can't buy rural land in China, but as agribusinesses and manufacturing companies have learned over the years, you can rent.

5

FOR RENT

Waiting for our host at Bodega Langes in Changli County, a three-hour drive east of Beijing, we knew it was a special place as we browsed through the wine shelves to see the lucky number eight in most prices. We saw one bottle for 888 yuan (well over a hundred dollars), another for 1,088, but the true eye-opener was the diamond-encrusted bottle, coming in at 180,000 yuan (over $26,000). An assistant invited us to sit at a nice conference table in the public reception area and kindly brought cold bottles of water. One of them exploded on us upon opening, but we deftly covered it up before anyone could see, because, you know, it was a classy place. We learned that the owner, Gernot Langes-Swarovski, was the Forbes billionaire owner of Bodega Norton in Argentina, and his grandfather had founded the Swarovski crystal brand. We couldn't help but wonder if the extra zeros in the price tag were a mistake.

Mr. Cui, the chief winemaker, was in a cheerful mood when he approached to greet us. His enthusiasm for the project, and the future of wine in China, was contagious—just what we needed for our first week in the country. Coming off paradoxically as both proud and unassuming at the same time, his thin frame added to a boyish squint that belied his middle-aged hairline and seemingly well-earned laugh lines. He thought aloud, filling his pauses with strings of "neiguh neiguh neiguh," a common Chinese filler word like the English *umm*, *like*, or *you know*. We listened carefully, partly because we didn't understand anything else until our assistant translated, but we also feel like understanding everyday words makes a new place seem a little more familiar.

Mr. Cui was in the first graduating class of a now-famous enology program near Xi'an. A winemaker before there was much domestic interest in wine, he spent a few years in agriculture. In 1999, he'd heard about a new place in Changli. Bodega Langes was set to open with a thirty-million-dollar investment, and they were looking for a winemaker. He'd been there ever since. In addition to chief winemaker, his business card boasted "state appraisal judge," a wine-tasting certification that let him travel, taste, and consult. His favorite wine? Opus One, from California, the most famous wine he'd ever tasted.

He walked us through the grounds, not slowly, but not in a hurry, patiently explaining details of the firm's cutting-edge winemaking technology. We could see why Opus One appealed. In the words of the fictional investor from Jurassic Park, "no expense was spared," which was less surprising once we'd seen the Swarovski crystal–encrusted bottle. Wine was made in a state-of-the-art gravity flow cellar system that treated the grapes more gently by letting gravity do the work. Instead of pumping the grapes into fermentation vats, grapes were crushed and destemmed on an upper level, letting the juice run down naturally to the next stop below.

The barrels were all Chinese oak, made by Bodega Langes's own cooperage business from forests in the north of China. It was a point of pride for Mr. Cui to use Chinese resources, and it was the only winery we knew to use Chinese oak, so we were intrigued. Few other winemakers had ever heard of it. We finally chatted with a barrel importer who offered an opinion. "It leaks," he explained. "A lot." So, you'll have loads of barrels of good wine, but you'll lose a lot too. We were never able to confirm this, but we also never saw another Chinese oak barrel, with the exception of an announcement that Ningxia's Changyu Moser was looking into it. Time will tell whether a local oak alternative is on the horizon.

The winery also had more basic equipment for recreational use by customers who'd cracked the fifty-thousand-yuan minimum purchase to become members. They could visit after harvest, put some boots on, and join their friends in the traditional foot-stomping extravaganza before spending the night at the winery hotel, overlooking the vines, eating and drinking to their hearts' content. Mr. Cui and his team would make each member's wine from their own crush. He loved educating visitors and budding wine enthusiasts. He explained that, at first, "they just 'ganbei!'"

chugging their glasses to toast, but later, they learned to pause and appreciate color, aroma, and taste.

Changli County, in Hebei Province, was an important early wine region, and as the industry emerged in the 1990s, the local government was looking for investors. Seduced by the project, and perhaps also by the owner's name and wealth, local authorities supported it. According to Mr. Cui, Bodega Langes was special because it wasn't just a "factory." Chinese farmers and winery employees made this distinction several times during our earlier visits. Wine "factories" buy grapes from farmers, and they "just" make the wine. They stay out of the risky business of grape growing. Bodega Langes was a "winery" because they controlled their grapes, more than two hundred hectares, spread across two fields. Curiosity mounted as we discussed the experimental area, with thirty trial varieties, including Malbec. "Only at Bodega Langes," said Mr. Cui, who had visited Argentina a few years earlier.

Remember that rural land is owned by village collectives, so you can't buy it. But even in a place already crowded with farms, there's a way around the tiny family plots problem: leasing from farmers. The winery rented plots from many individual farmers and consolidated them into a coherent vineyard that could be farmed with hired labor. In this kind of deal, companies have their "own" farm in the sense that for the duration of the lease, they rent the farmers' use rights over the land. Then, the company calls the shots in the farm, making it much easier to obtain consistent quality than by dealing with independent growers on informal contracts.

Bodega Langes had an in-house program to train winery staff, who were often graduates from university wine programs, so that they could, in turn, teach the farmers what to do. Mr. Cui explained that growers needed consistent training in order to follow instructions, especially with experimental varietals or more complicated tasks. Wages varied according to the task. For weeding, farmers were paid based on the distance covered, but for other vineyard management tasks, they received an hourly or daily rate. Some farmers accepted the new rules easily, he told us, but others were harder to convince. Remember, they'd been working this land a lot longer than the winery had been around, and the staff members were still outsiders.

As long as farmers were paid good rents, it could be a good deal for them. They no longer worried about agricultural risk because their wages didn't depend on grape quality. They got income from their land, even in a bad vintage. And they could take another job, often as workers for the winery itself, to earn more money.

Put like this, the land-lease approach to vineyard management seemed like such a clear win-win that we wondered why everybody wasn't doing it, especially since it had been a common way to scale up farms for other crops. In Hebei, Mr. Cui said the government increasingly encouraged wineries to apply for their own land allocation directly from the government. Maybe the whole win-win thing wasn't quite as easy as it sounded.

* * *

Did you know China is the largest apple producer in the world? In 2013, it produced more than thirty-one million tons of apples, almost ten times more than the runner up, the United States, and accounted for half of the world's output.[1] The country went from being a net importer to a net exporter in just twenty years, and by 2013, a quarter of all apples in the world came from just three Chinese provinces. Exporters avoided so-called high-end markets like Europe or the United States because of strict standards on things such as pesticide residue, but agro-industry was exploding right alongside other major sectors.

One of those megagrowers was Shandong Province, where wine and wine tourism began. Apple growing took many forms. There were, of course, agribusinesses working with small independent growers, just as Grace Vineyard and Yunnan Hong did with grapes. Some farmers sold apples to buyers who showed up just before harvest, with little to no other involvement. But larger growing operations were those that, like Bodega Langes, had patched up an orchard thanks to leasing many small farmers' plots.[2] Land leases of this kind allowed agribusinesses to scale up despite the prohibition against land purchase. For some, it could improve agricultural productivity and create new, nonfarm opportunities for farmers, without disturbing the politically sensitive collective ownership of rural land.

But for farmers, it was much riskier than it appeared at Bodega Langes. Due to the lack of individual ownership, and the power of village authorities in regular land reallocations, families were concerned that if they stopped farming themselves and rented out their plot, they might never get it back.[3] In some villages, there was a rule that land left uncultivated for a period of time had to be reallocated. In theory, you could move to a city to find a better job and keep your land productive back home by renting it. But informal contracts are notoriously hard to enforce, so you can imagine why farmers might be hesitant to rent, even if it meant leaving opportunities unexploited.

The lease terms are shakier than it seems for the winery too. Do you remember the wonderful up-and-coming agri-tourism village of Mulangou, in Shandong? The Scottish Castle controlled its vineyard thanks to a fifty-year lease of many farmers' small plots. And you know who else moved into the village and benefited from a similar arrangement? Lafite, the uber famous wine name from Bordeaux. Domaines Barons de Rothschild, the group that owns Chateau Lafite, had chosen Mulangou to establish its first Chinese winery. Of course, these arrangements depended on the local government to help coordinate the many individual transactions involved. Organizing the deal was never easy, Gérard Colin remembered. He worked with the Scottish Castle and then with Lafite when they started in 2009. We'd been told to keep an eye out for the cute street sign to the "French Cottage," so we smiled when we passed Gérard's old house next to an outdoor public gym, just as we entered Mulangou for the first time.

Gérard explained the process with nostalgia and a bemused hint at the frustration he must have felt at the time. At first, you negotiate with the government and they say there's no problem. It looks as if you've got a deal. But then, you talk to farmers individually to get planting. He finished the sentence with a wry chuckle. It turns out not everyone had agreed. To this day, patches of other crops are scattered around the Scottish Castle vineyard, plots the farmers had never wanted to rent out, no matter what the local government had said. We wondered what the negotiations had really entailed, who got paid how much, and when and how transparent (or not) the deals had been between farmers and local officials.

Of course, a lot depends on local politics. The government coordinates the lease, manages agreements with farmers, and plays a key role in the terms for both sides. There's a reason coordinated leases don't happen everywhere. Shandong and Hebei are very wealthy, fertile regions. Agricultural land is far more valuable there, and it's likely that every available mu is already being cultivated. It might not be a coincidence that local governments came to the rescue in places with more money and eager foreign investors, especially if "no expense was spared."

Farmers work on green harvest at Lafite, a common practice for commercial wineries that is counterintuitive for subsistence farmers.

So how secure are these arrangements? No one knows what will happen when the lease expires in fifty years, but you might think they're safe until then. Not so fast. Something bigger had already come to Mulangou. From a visit in 2016, we learned that very soon, the village would enjoy a convenient . . . highway. It was part of a road project linking the south of Shandong and Manchuria, where a few hectares of vines, including Lafite's, would be sacrificed. We thought Lafite might be powerful enough to stop this, given its name and its then business partner, the state-owned construction company CITIC. But the wine deals were with local authorities, and the road project came from higher up.[4] Maybe things were easier in a place with more uncultivated land and a lot less rain. To find out, let's head back to the place everyone was talking about: Ningxia Hui Autonomous Region.

* * *

Silver Heights winery, on the outskirts of Yinchuan, the capital of Ningxia, was already one of the most famous wineries in China, but it wasn't easy to find on this sunny morning in 2013. Our taxi driver had understood the address perfectly well, and he had even spoken to the owner on the phone as we got closer. Still, the driver ended up leaving us at an unfinished bridge, and we walked the rest of the way on a dirt road after crossing a little canal. Given that customers visited the house directly to buy wine every day, we imagined that this little piece of urban sprawl might be frustrating for a family winery. Luckily, famous critics around the world kept coming back, concluding that this little urban farmhouse winery was making some of the best wine in China.

We were greeted by the head of the Silver Heights operation, Bordeaux-trained winemaker Emma Gao. She welcomed us warmly, and it was easy to see how this kind, pretty smile, cute bob, and comfortable shirt reflect the multifaceted lifestyle of a powerful businesswoman, a famous winemaker, and a mom who did a lot of her work from home. We were eager for her story. We knew she'd done a prestigious internship at Chateau Calon Ségur in the Médoc. It was there that she fell in love with the easygoing, sandy-haired maître de chai, Thierry Courtade. Many years later, her now-husband Thierry had long-since moved to Yinchuan to make wine with her.

Their daughter, little eight-year-old Emma, joined us as we tasted a blend of Cabernet Sauvignon and Cabernet Gernischt (a grape recently found to be Carmenere). She gleefully introduced us to the farm's rabbits, pony, and goats, explaining how she wanted to be a veterinarian when she grew up. But she's a winemaker's daughter, and she already had a remarkably sophisticated palate. She grabbed her mom's Riedel glass, swirled with confidence, sniffed, and in the same strong southern accent as her dad, said in French, "It smells like chocolate milk." "Yes," Mom said, with unmistakable pride in her voice as she looked from her daughter to us, "chocolate because of the oak barrel, and milk because of the malolactic fermentation. Very good, *ma chérie.*"

Until recently, all their wine was made at this small family farm, where they grew a few wine grapes, table grapes for sale, and vegetables for home consumption. Small fermentation tanks were spread over three underground cellars dug by Emma's father. In wine speak, you would call that a true *garagiste* operation. But the property was threatened by urban sprawl and the construction of some sort of music-themed public park, which was the cause of our troubles getting there that morning.

We talked about where they got their grapes and how they envisioned the future, particularly limited by their small plot of a little over fifty hectares. Unsurprisingly, part of their success was built supplementing their own grapes by contracting with a couple of trusted independent growers. For the winemaking couple, the Silver Heights team was never more than a few employees, nowhere near enough to coordinate leases or large groups of farmers. Instead, they nurtured a few key relationships and labored to convince higher-ups that they were worthy of more.

Emma brought out architectural plans for a new, bigger winery they planned to build at the foot of the Helan Mountain. But they were still working on the long process of convincing the local government to allocate the land they would need. At this point, there was plenty of unallocated land and excitement about wine, particularly at the provincial government, but there were also swarms of eager stakeholders, and it was unclear what would garner the most support. Emma's father and sister had been doing quite a bit of this negotiation behind the scenes, and we were happy to come back and visit the new winery and new vines that were up and running in 2015.

Everyone in Ningxia told us that local government support made good winemaking possible, but obviously it was still complicated. Sure, maybe behemoth wineries didn't struggle to get land. State-owned giant Xixia King had no trouble planting two thousand hectares when it sought to expand production in Ningxia. And the multinational giant Moët & Chandon had plenty of government land, though it still bought in half of its grapes when we visited in 2015. But there, relationships with farmers were relatively straightforward. When we asked our host the hardest part of his job, he didn't skip a beat before he said "relationships with the government."

If you believe that great wine is made in the vineyard, then quality is all about the land. There were several boutique wineries that, like Silver Heights, were committed to very high quality. More and more, Ningxia was the place to be, attracting investors from everywhere. Remember Grace Vineyard from Shanxi? When they wanted to expand but continue to ensure the best grapes, they applied for land in Ningxia and sent a vineyard manager, Mr. Cai, to run it. They didn't have much (barely even a winery in Ningxia), but they had an established business plan, the right contacts, and enough investment capital to convince the local government to give them more than sixty-five hectares. That was enough that Grace could diversify its production and even cooperate with other winemakers to expand, experiment, and see if they could explore terroir in Ningxia.

One of those winemaking pals was Bordeaux-trained expert Zhang Yanzhi. He was able to get his Ningxia vineyard up and running, but it takes years to get a good harvest and time to develop relationships with farmers. So, while he worked on getting the best grapes from farmers with older vines (including paying them a hearty premium for the highest-quality grapes), he also convinced Mr. Cai to sell him grapes from some of Grace Vineyard's four-year-old vines.

More and more, Ningxia vineyard land was cultivated by farmers who knew how to grow quality grapes (and were paid for them). And the local government was connecting investors, winemakers, and vineyard managers to make wine with the right resources and expertise to impress even the most demanding consumers. So, it seemed as if nothing could stop Ningxia.

Except . . . well, one of the things that makes Ningxia great for wine grapes is that hot, dry climate, combined with irrigation from the Yellow River. When a couple of wineries become a couple hundred wineries, could there really be enough water for everybody?

* * *

It was the summer of 2015 and Yanzhi's import business kept him busy in Beijing. He spent time at his Guanlan vineyard near Yinchuan whenever he could, but he'd hired a thirtysomething young winemaker, Liao, to oversee the operations full time. Like so many in the Chinese wine industry, Liao, too, is a graduate from the college of enology near Xi'an. He'd cut his winemaker teeth at Grace Vineyard before landing a gig in Australia as a junior winemaker. It was during his time in Australia that he really learned the importance of vineyard work. He still loves Grace and speaks fondly of his time there. He told us he tried to visit regularly and often checked online to order Grace's latest releases.

Liao lived in the office that Yanzhi rented in a nice neighborhood of Yinchuan. But he couldn't wait to live in the middle of the vineyard once the winery was built. When you're in the city, he explained, the city owns you. He preferred the clean air and quiet of the vineyard. You can still see the city from afar, he noted. His friends joked he needed a girlfriend. On the way to the Guanlan site, his analytical eye couldn't help but pick apart other vineyards: "It's very bad here, I don't like it. Oh, this one is OK, and that over there is very good." He didn't hesitate to point out needed improvements in Guanlan's vineyard too. Those baby Cabernet Sauvignon vines imported from France, he explained—they're very good, just so much stronger than those that came from a local nursery, located in the other block.

In this new wine area of Jinshan, with breathtaking views at the foot of Helan Mountain, thirty or so winery projects were underway. Much of the area still looked like a bunch of rocks, but grapevines were starting to come along, gradually turning the dry landscape into something greener. And they all needed plenty of water. As Mike Veseth, the Wine Economist, once put it, when Jesus turned water into wine, perhaps the real miracle was that he didn't waste a drop. Have you ever thought about how much water it takes to make a liter of wine? According to Waterfootprint.org, the global average need is 870 liters. It's not as bad as the water footprint of a hamburger, but you can see why in wine regions that have been hit by drought, such as California and Australia, water is a very serious matter.

Guanlan Vineyard.

Traditionally, farmers used flood irrigation, but for Jinshan, the authorities subsidized a more controlled and sustainable drip irrigation system. To provide water for wineries, the government funded two shared reservoirs drawing water from the Yellow River. At first, officials had planned to convince a farmer to give up some land for the reservoirs. We think there's something optimistic about the fact that the owner successfully refused to give it up, not wanting to waste any of his plot. Meanwhile, Yanzhi was more than happy to volunteer some acreage, eager to have a water source conveniently located right behind his vineyard.

Summers are hot and dry in Ningxia. Without irrigation from the Yellow River, there would be no agriculture. Growth in the local economy also meant draining a scarce resource. So, while we were excited about the big wine tourism projects, sustainability remained concerning. It didn't help that one of the leading industries in Ningxia was coal mining, a very thirsty business, and not just a problem for Ningxia. As cities along the Yellow River grow and consume, they leave less water for people downstream. The government made some laudable strides, particularly putting a stop to the recurring failure of the river to reach the sea in the 1990s.[5] Still, it's hard to imagine how northern China's residents and industries can scale back the pressure on one river.

Instead of getting in the messy business of regulating demand, the Chinese government has been keener to address supply. Extraordinary engineering projects channeled water from the wetter South toward northern regions, which have a tiny percentage of the country's water but about half of its people. By the time of our research, Ningxia's coal mining had long since surpassed its water quota, and the local economy showed no signs of slowing. At some point, it seems that regulators will have to address demand.[6]

The problem when we visited wasn't just the hot and dry summers. Ningxia is a desert region with brutal winters, where farmers buried vines by hand right after harvest to beat the annual and deadly cold front. Unfortunately, burying meant scarce water and labor. Vineyard managers lamented the entire process. One farmer would push down the heavily watered trunk, so that another could cover it with dirt. Anyone without enough water or dirt to protect the vines would be in for a bad surprise in the spring. "That happened to a couple of wineries nearby," Liao explained. Many of their vines had not survived the winter.

With dozens of new wineries in the works, eventually the water constraint will hit hard in Ningxia. But there is some hope. Maybe, just maybe, wineries can be part of the solution. At least that's what the Asian Development Bank (ADB) seemed to think. ADB had an ongoing project to support more sustainable irrigation in local agriculture.[7] And check out this part of the strategy: "to increase the quality of grapes while reducing volume, through planting of the Project Crops and application of drip irrigation technology." Next, ADB hoped to help with marketing those new, higher-quality wines. Promoting fine wine to save the planet—clever! But wait. Farther west, there's a much, much drier place, where local officials we met were also betting on wine for economic development.

* * *

Gérard Colin really was the Indiana Jones of winemakers. In 2014, we met him at his new winemaking gig, near Turpan in Xinjiang. The owner, from Hong Kong, had made his fortune with a company selling minidisks in Shenzhen. Later, he sold it and went into real estate and the stock market. We don't know how he came across this little winery, Puchang, but here it was, on a quiet and unremarkable road on the outskirts of Turpan. He must have gotten some support, because the municipal government was keen to develop the local wine industry, including wine tourism. Tourists come to Turpan for the heritage tourism sites, to learn about Uighur culture, ride camels, or take pictures in front of the Flaming Mountains, which are supposed to look as if they're on fire. Wine tourism is a natural development, since the region is already known for grapes, raisins, and wine. One of the local tourist attractions is the Grape Valley, a park devoted to grapevines. We were amazed by the diversity of raisins available at markets. So many different colors, textures, and aromas, they almost dwarfed the sundried tomatoes.

To bring the wines up to the next level, Puchang's owner hired Gérard, playing up the Lafite experience on the website, and a well-traveled Italian winemaker, Loris Tartaglia. They both lived on the property, each in their little room with air-conditioning and a shared bathroom. "It's our little prison," they joked, referring to the isolation of the winery as well as the cement walls. Gérard and Loris were energized by the challenge of practicing their craft in extreme conditions.

By the evening, our fingers were thoroughly messy from barbecued lamb skewers at an outdoor restaurant. After making funny faces and blowing raspberries, Gérard put down the baby he'd met at a table nearby and picked up a cigarette. Although he enjoyed the new world of people and food far from his adopted home in Shandong, Gérard told us he planned to leave Xinjiang after this contract. "Making wine in a Muslim region for government customers—I just don't want to do that."

He didn't pull punches about the prices paid to farmers either. We took notes as a coworker explained, "There are no yield limits, so farmers can grow as much as they want."

"No," Gérard fired back with the tone of calm authority that professors call a "teaching moment." "The problem is that wineries don't want to pay." He went on: "The most expensive wine in China costs forty yuan per bottle to make. The rest is marketing." One good bottle takes about a kilo of grapes, so, he argued, wineries can afford the premium price of six to ten yuan per kilo instead of the typical four yuan.

This observation was hardly surprising, but we also wanted to know what was unique about southern Xinjiang, with its distinctive history and politics. We explored the area and met with "Luke," another foreign winemaker who had lived in Xinjiang for many years. Until recently, the winery he worked for had contracted with groups of local farmers, but never with individuals. Managing the grape supply in this way was more "poetic" and harder to monitor. For example, he explained, "You may agree on five yuan per kilo in advance, but once the harvest comes, a competitor shows up offering eight. In that case, you've lost your grapes, and even if there was a contract, there is very little they can do to enforce it. You can really sign all kinds of contracts with farmers."

The winery had shifted toward purchasing its grapes from "regiment" groups of farmers, known as the XPCC. In the 1950s, under Mao Tse Tung, thousands of Han settlers (China's majority ethnic group) were sent to Xinjiang to secure the border from the Soviet Union and promote economic development. They became farmers but also serve as a reserve army in case of war. Luke pointed out that they must have gotten rusty as soldiers, wondering how these soldiers-cum-farmers would fare in the event of an actual war.

We were often interested in topics we weren't in a position to discuss openly. In the same way that farmers hesitated to criticize wineries, almost everyone hesitated to discuss social and political tensions. Still, we wondered how the regiment groups were perceived in the local Uighur Muslim community, given vast economic and social inequality, as well as important political tension in the region. Scholars refer to the regiment group as a direct attempt to "stabilize" Xinjiang with Han residents,[8] noting early "harsh measures"[9] designed to control the local population. We could believe the official claim that there are now members from many different ethnic and religious groups, but you'll forgive us if we take some of the official account with a grain of salt: "Carrying out the central government's policies toward ethnic groups and religions in an all-round way, the XPCC handles religious affairs in accordance with the law, and has become a large, united, multi-ethnic family."[10]

In any case, we learned that each of these units is a close-knit community, where the regiment provides public services like education, health care, and security. And importantly, they supervise agricultural production. Luke explained logically that the military-style chain of command makes them easier to work with than regular farmer groups because the head of a regiment gives orders based on the specifics provided by the winery, and the team follows orders. It probably helps that they don't have to worry about feeding their families.

Whether it's contracts, land, or weather, everyone in wine stays up at night worrying about quality grapes. Thankfully, no one in Turpan worried about getting them ripe. Just south of the Tian Shan Mountains, annual rainfall is half an inch or less. This means intensely ripe grapes well before the winter burying. Plus, it's so hot and dry that most insects and diseases can be avoided. No pesticides needed here. Gérard Colin's Puchang wines were certified organic by the Ecocert Group. But . . . the water.

Even though we'd read about it, we couldn't help but be perplexed when we saw the green oasis of the grape corridor that made Turpan an important stop on the Silk Road. The trick is an ingenious ancient system of irrigation that channels snow melt from the Tian Shan Mountains through wells and canals to the farmland where it's needed for agriculture. The system is called *Karez*, the namesake of our beautiful hotel in Turpan. It all moves by sheer gravity, through underground canals that prevent too much evaporation along the way. That was great for generations of subsistence farmers, but it is hardly an abundant source for industry.

The Xinjiang government regulated access strictly, especially for agriculture. Vegetable planting was severely restricted to keep more water available to local industry, but wineries we visited couldn't simply turn it

Desert architecture in the perplexingly lush grape corridor.

on when they needed it. Each business representative had to make a phone call in the morning to get in line and hope for the best. If the water didn't come, a producer might call again and again, only to find out that despite all the "yes, it's coming" answers they'd heard in the morning, they would have to wait until the next day. Of course, grapes without enough water will shrivel long before they can ripen.

The problem was so obvious that we weren't surprised to find a World Bank project to help farmers,[11] including a transition from flood irrigation to a more sustainable modern drip system. Of course, drip irrigation can't solve everything. In Shanshan, ninety minutes east of Turpan, the soil is sandy and . . . salty. Soil salinity is bad for plant growth, so you need to reduce it by flushing the salts out, which, we were told, could only happen with flood irrigation.

When we learned about the municipal government's plan to build one hundred new wineries in Turpan by 2020, we had to wonder where they'd get the water. The Chinese government often has new ambitious plans to increase the water supply in the dry North. We have to pause at the way these announcements are reported, as if there were no people currently using the abundant, yet distant, water sources. Here in Xinjiang, we learned the reprieve might come from thousands of miles away in the Bohai Sea.[12] The plan was to build a pipeline to pump seawater on the northeast coast and bring it to the Northwest. Then, put it through a desalination plant at the destination, and voilà! Impressive from an engineering standpoint, but this kind of grandiose project is very controversial. Environmental groups point out the ecological risks as well as the large displacement of populations involved. The difficult question of how to regulate demand will have to be addressed, especially as more land gets leased to wineries in dry western regions.

* * *

Guan Youjiang and his family will probably remember September 30, 2008, for the rest of their lives. He was among the group of eighteen who, thirty years earlier, had signed the secret document in Xiaogang. It must have been quite something to sit down in front of his house and chat with General Secretary Hu Jintao. Two weeks later, the Communist Party was going to discuss rural reforms at the Third Plenary Session of the Seventeenth Central Committee. Sitting in Youjiang's courtyard, with bowls of local fruits and peanuts within easy reach, Hu Jintao reassured villagers that "the current contract relationship is stable and will not change in the long term."[13] So much for those in international media who had anxiously awaited the privatization of farmland. But Hu did take a step in the direction of landownership. Farmers would be allowed to lease or transfer their land-use rights in an official rural land market (a bit like the one Bodega Langes had been using for a decade).

Of course, villagers throughout China had already been doing this for a while in various creative ways, exploiting the ambiguity of land laws.[14] As one Beijing professor of land management puts it, "In China, before the law changes there are always going to be a lot of local experiments."[15] Chinese winemakers will have to make do with some trial and error, getting the best grapes by finding what works in each local environment. You might say that's what winemakers always try to do. It's just that they might not realize that terroir, that unique sense of place, is as important in politics as it is in vineyards. For the moment, they have demonstrated that you can get good wine grapes in a Chinese vineyard even if it's unclear what will happen when leases expire or when the water supplies just can't keep up with eager new investors. Interestingly, the uncertainty hasn't stopped foreign investors from settling in to make Chinese wine themselves. And with so many new successful wineries, there is room for new research, innovation, and new crops of students with enology degrees.

6

BACK TO SCHOOL

We had just checked in at the Hyatt hotel on the University of California Davis campus, a short walk from the famous Department of Viticulture and Enology. Our mission on this short spring break trip: "Understanding Jiu," as promised by the title of an exciting symposium. *Jiu* is the generic term for alcohol in Chinese. Topics included wine, of course, but also beer brewing in China, Chinese grain wines and spirits, archeological evidence of ancient fermented beverages, and the place of *jiu* in Chinese literature. Soon after our arrival at the hotel, we noticed a group of exhausted Chinese visitors waiting with their luggage in the lounge. One man in his late fifties got up to smoke a cigarette outside. "Look, it's Li Hua!" said Pierre. We were starstruck. That "wine college near Xi'an" everybody kept telling us they came from—he founded it. Here he was, casually dressed, after a long journey that made his hair look as if he'd just gotten out of bed.

The next evening, after a fun day of presentations, a young Chinese woman, one of Davis's graduate students in viticulture and enology, approached us during the symposium dinner. "Excuse me, my professors have heard you are from Washington. They would like to meet you." She led us to the other side of the teaching winery, where dinner was held, next to the high-tech fermentation tanks Davis students use to develop their chops. Here we were, starstruck, even more this time, standing in front of Li Hua; his wife and colleague, Wang Hua; and their associate, Dr. Fang Yulin. Their last stop on this trip would be Washington State University, before catching their flight home from Seattle. The following week, we picked them up at their airport hotel and took them out to dinner at Toulouse Petit, a fun place for shareable plates of Cajun-Creole cuisine and seafood in the Queen Anne neighborhood. English had been our only dinner language. But that was until Dr. Li tilted his glass of Washington Sauvignon Blanc to pour one drop into the fresh oyster he was holding in the other hand. "C'est ce que je faisais à Bordeaux," he said in perfect French. After all, he'd started his wine journey in Bordeaux, where local oysters are classically paired with the region's crisp white wines made of Sauvignon Blanc.

After a bachelor of science in agronomy at Sichuan Agricultural College, he left for France in 1982 to pursue a master's and PhD in viticulture and enology at the University of Bordeaux. He didn't speak much French before going, but he learned quickly, pushed by the rigorous demands of his studies and boosted further by extracurricular activities. He played soccer and, of course, ping-pong. After completing his PhD, he returned to China to become an academic and conduct research on grape growing and winemaking, and eventually founded the College of Enology at Northwest Agricultural and Forestry University, in Yangling, a ninety-minute drive from Xi'an in Shaanxi Province. For Yanzhi and his young colleague Liao in Ningxia, Mr. Cui at Bodega Langes in Hebei, and many others, Yangling was where the professional wine journey started.

We will never forget our Toulouse Petit dinner, first because Li Hua and his colleagues are such wonderful and knowledgeable people, but also because of what we failed to prevent from happening at the end. Dr. Li grabbed a creamy chunk a little smaller than a golf ball from one of the plates. As his Bordeaux friends would, he felt it was time for a little cheese course. It was just nanoseconds before the fork reached his mouth that Cynthia realized what was happening. "That's not cheese!" Cynthia exclaimed. But too late. Dr. Li nodded, valiantly controlling his gag reflex. We call it the butter incident.

It was fitting that we met Li Hua and his colleagues for the first time at one of the world's meccas for winemakers' training. In the years following the repeal of Prohibition, research and teaching at Davis's Department of Viticulture and Enology were key to developing the quality and commercial viability of California's wine industry. Decades later, you are likely to meet the department's sought-after graduates at many wineries around the world. A wine industry, wherever it is, needs well-trained professionals and input from scientific research. At the University of Bordeaux, prominent academics like Pascal Ribéreau-Gayon and Emile Peynaud produced pioneering research that shaped modern winemaking. In South Africa, research institutes helped spread ideas about the importance of site selection and effective vineyard management so that grape growers could adopt them. In Chile, universities passed on knowledge to local wineries, helping them become exporters.[1] Thanks to the clout of his Bordeaux PhD, scientific research, and involvement in the emerging industry, Li Hua scaled up what was the first wine program in Asia, and it is still the largest and most prestigious. Faculty and students there like to say that there are two kinds of people in the Chinese wine industry: those who graduated from Northwest and those who didn't. A few months after the butter incident, at last, we were standing in front of that "wine college near Xi'an" where so many of the people we had met all around China came from, whether they were winemakers, cellar lab assistants, or importers.

* * *

Lurong was beginning her senior year when her good spoken English got her on duty to pick us up at Xi'an airport. Poor Lurong arrived early and had to wait for hours as our flight was delayed. She used to go by "Lareina" in English but later decided it was too complicated, so she changed it to Anne. Her family had no interest in wine. She chose the major out of curiosity and because wine sounded like a great way to learn about the world and travel. Like Lurong, most students at the college majored in viticulture and enology, but a quarter focused on wine marketing. In the end, in fact, as many as 80 percent of graduates ended up in wine business careers rather than becoming winemakers. Lurong knew her way around grapevines and fermentation tanks, but she was interested in a business career, perhaps even wine writing and journalism. She preferred New World wines, with bold, fruity aromas, she explained. "Maybe it's because I'm young. When I'm thirty, forty, maybe I'll like French wines," she said. She did have a soft spot for Italian wines though, because they always surprised her. In fact, she wrote her senior thesis on the market for Italian wine in China.

Why Italy? It all started when she took a popular wine culture and appreciation course with Denise, a well-traveled Italian wine consultant with degrees from Bordeaux and Montpelier in France. She and her partner, Alessio, also a wine consultant and wine business teacher at the college, had been lecturing in Yangling for a couple of years when we visited. "They travel the world and make wine together. They are the *perfect couple!*" said Lurong, with a dreamy look in the distance. A few weeks after graduation, Lurong was living the dream, a three-month internship at a winery in the Lazio region of Italy, thanks to her favorite Italian professors. Her Italian wine adventure could certainly be one of the defining moments in her career. The perfect couple was on to something when it came to promoting the wines of their homeland. As part of their degree, students did internships during the winter and summer months. Most stayed in China, of course, but a lucky few went abroad. They were trained to work in the vineyard, the cellar, and the lab. But most eventually wanted jobs on the business side, often ending up working for importers.

The business side of wine offered better jobs and pay, and more exciting locations, in big cities, rather than life in dark cellars and remote vineyards. So, in addition to wine scientists, the college had a strong wine marketing research and teaching group, led by Professor Li Jiagui. Jiagui taught his specialty, wine marketing, in a course that started from marketing theory and then applied the principles to various wine case studies of the world. He'd been at the university for a long time. After his BA in economics, he took a teaching position at Li Hua's then three-year-old college of enology. Over the years, he moved up the academic ranks, earning his master's in management in 2005 and culminating with a PhD in 2014. An associate professor at the college of enology, he led the wine marketing group, including a freshly hired wine entrepreneurship expert, Li Huanmei, with a PhD from Australia.

"This is very good wine," he commented after a big sip of Ningxia red wine he'd brought to share at dinner. He added, "Everybody knows there is very good wine in China. But this one is three hundred yuan; it's too expensive. Maybe if it's two hundred, it's OK." Jiagui had a point. Inflated prices were a common problem for many of the best Chinese wines to compete effectively with imports. Perhaps the wine marketing research conducted by Jiagui's team, covering topics like wine consumption trends among Chinese youth, wine tourism, online wine sales, or how to market wine better to the younger generation, could help give Chinese wineries a reality check.

A few months after our first visit, the wine college moved to a new, more modern building, with improved facilities for students' hands-on winemaker training. It was all up and running when we came back to Yangling a year later, and the dean gave us the tour.

* * *

Dressed comfortably in jeans and a sweater, Dr. Wang Hua could be a liberal arts college professor in the laid-back US Pacific Northwest. She lived with her husband, college founder Li Hua, in a lovely ground-floor apartment near the university in Yangling. She chose the floor strategically, so that she could make "Dr. Li Hua," as she referred to him when speaking English, step outside to smoke one of the many cigarettes he got through every day. About ten years ago, she took over as dean of the college. As we walked in the dining hall, she smiled as she greeted three young women in lab coats. "Wang Laoshi!" (Professor Wang!), said one of the students, clearly happy to see her. Students felt comfortable around her. The dining hall was crowded with students inside, and dozens of open umbrellas sat outside the front door. Welcome to the food court of our dreams, the kind where there is so much variety that you could debate whether the stuffed flatbread station offered the version from Tianjin or Shandong, before moving on to decide between spicy buckwheat noodle soup or steamed noodles with fish. Dean Wang cared about giving us a tour around all the stations first to explain every detail, and we marveled at the efficiency of the staff behind each stall, tossing fresh ingredients in hot woks and assembling stuffed breads and soups to order.

"If you want to know the university, you have to eat here. This is where you can know the students," said Dean Wang as we sat down with our food. From the very first time we stepped into the college of enology, we were struck by how much the faculty cared about building relationships with students and alumni. There always seemed to be students in professors' offices, or professors excusing themselves because they were on their way to lunch with students. As we toured the new building where the college had just moved in, Dean Wang greeted every single student she passed, calling them by name and then telling us about their research. Each year, the college of enology admits 120 first-year students.

The new building, marked with the Chinese name of the college in big yellow font, was impressive. Wang Laoshi's eyes were filled with pride as we stood behind the lab in progress. Students in white coats were working in pairs, practicing their wine lab technician chops in a new classroom laboratory big enough to accommodate the whole class of 2018. On one table, empty bottles of Chinese and imported wines left over from tasting classes served as containers for students' experiments. And their training wasn't confined to the lab. These students were preparing to use their skills on wine they would make themselves a few weeks later. Every year, under the guidance of professors, students worked the school vineyard, harvested grapes, and drove them in through a garage door going straight into the winemaking facility just behind the lab. Some grapes were immediately sorted, crushed, destemmed, and loaded in one of the dozens of one-hundred-liter fermenters, while others waited for their turn as students' guinea pigs in the adjacent cold chamber. The budding winemakers could experiment with different fermentation temperatures, thanks to a system of pipes sending water around the tanks to cool or warm them.

Most of the funding for all this came from the government. To obtain any equipment, from simple desks to temperature-controlled tanks, the college applied to the university first and, once approved, organized an auction where suppliers bid to get the contract. The lowest bidder won, although, Dean Wang explained, she and her colleagues could make the case to the university when they preferred to pay more for better quality. That was how they got the tanks, all made in China by the company that supplied equipment to one of China's wine giants, Great Wall winery.

Yangling College of Enology students working hard in lab class.

Each tank had a sticker with the name of the company, and students could scan a QR code to learn more about them. The company was happy to be a supplier, even at a low price, because it was good for public relations. Many students would work in the industry, and they'd remember the name from their school days.

Li Hua had founded the college and brought it to fame, but Dean Wang wanted to continue moving it forward. Under her leadership, faculty-student relations improved dramatically. When she hired new professors, she insisted they must care about students, and not just about their research. Along the way, she promoted school spirit in creative ways. In the entrance hall by the elevators, standing by a wall with dozens of plaques indicating amounts of money and donors' names, she enthusiastically explained various awards students could win. Donors included professors, alumni, a student's parent, a supplier of winemaking equipment, and an importer of Australian and New Zealand wines. The most fun and surprising prize was the "Wang Hua Number One" award. She created it, provided the seed donation of one hundred thousand yuan, and other donors followed. The idea was to support students beyond school, in "the development of the whole person," she said with conviction. If a student, alone or with a team of classmates from the college, entered a competition in anything (bridge tournament, dancing, ping-pong, etc.) and won the top spot, they could apply for "Wang Hua Number One" to receive one hundred yuan per team member. Another award, the Li Hua prize, was for those who turned a research paper into a publication in a scholarly journal. There was even an award for graduates who had been working at the same company for three years. Dr. Wang understood the importance of school spirit and an engaged alumni network. Successful alumni were in a position to give back to the college they loved, offer internships, or simply come back to visit and give lectures to share their experience with current students.

Many students craved a more global understanding of the wine world. Professors organized tastings and seminars with invited speakers. Sometimes, the guests were academics and wine educators, but there were also visits by promoters of famous wine regions. Students did their own wine homework too. Once a week, motivated classmates got together as a tasting group. One student collected the money and bought the selected wines online, and then the group met in the college's tasting classroom to sample a dozen different wines of the world. Older graduates remembered it was more difficult back in their day, when students learned all the motions in the cellar, but without much experience tasting wines of the world, they lacked clear models to improve their craft. Thanks to the extreme convenience of Chinese online shopping (more on that later), students could now have the world of wine delivered to their dorm.

Beyond tasting, Dean Wang and her colleagues were passionate about creating new opportunities for students. That's why they were in California where we met for the first time. After the symposium at UC Davis, they were off to Fresno State University, where they had a partnership. Selected students, after completing their first three years in Yangling, could earn a scholarship to spend the next two years in the Fresno wine program and then return home to defend their thesis research. They stopped by Washington State before going home to seal the deal on a new program with Washington State University: selected third-year Chinese winemakers in training would be able to complete their last two years at WSU. A shorter but exciting program took a group of twenty to thirty undergraduates abroad to visit a wine region for a few weeks during the summer. Students paid half of the cost, and the university sponsored the rest. For many, this was their first time abroad.

While some government scholarships were available, most students still couldn't afford traveling outside the country. And of course, another major challenge to studying abroad was the language barrier. Fortunately, there was no shortage of wineries in China looking for qualified interns and employees, so students could gain experience at home. In fact, there were two especially memorable wineries within a two-hour drive from Yangling. Let's take a break from school to visit them.

* * *

Sep 12, 2015, Saturday
AM 8:00–12:00, visit the Chateau in Xianyang
PM 15:35, departure, from Xi'an to Fuzhou, FM 8212, 15:35–18:05

This was the itinerary that wine marketing professor Li Jiagui had printed for the end of our first visit to Yangling. What was that "visit the Chateau in Xianyang"? The chateau in question was located a convenient fifteen-minute drive to Xi'an airport, so we wouldn't have to worry about missing our flight. What could there possibly be so close to the airport? Well, there's a big (very big) chateau, we discovered, as we got out of the van.

After two intense days visiting the school and giving a guest lecture, it felt like spring break.

Jiagui looked relaxed and happy as he greeted the young front desk staff, all in matching costumes. "Li Laoshi!" (Professor Li!) they exclaimed in unison with bright smiles. Most were his former students. Welcome to Chateau Changyu Reina, another one of Changyu's extravagant castles, designed for visitors to "Dream of Italy," the brochure said. At the time, we had never set foot in Italy, so Changyu Reina was the first Italian castle we'd ever seen. The honorary president, Augusto Reina, was the CEO of a major Italian conglomerate with a large wines and spirits division.

The tour started with the usual Changyu fun: history, museum to the glory of the brand, and the interactive games area designed to engage all your senses. But that was just the beginning, and the property was big enough that we rode to the next part in an open-air little van, snapping pictures of vineyards, fountains, and statues at every turn. We had not even been to Changyu Moser yet, the French Renaissance castle in Ningxia. You might remember Moser had a 3-D Globe movie theater, an impressive enough amenity for a winery. So, imagine our surprise when, at Reina, we put on glasses and stepped in a . . . 4-D theater. After we buckled our seatbelts (important), lights went off, seats elevated and started shaking, and off we were. The animated film began with a young couple on a date at the Changyu wine culture museum in Yantai, on the east coast, where Chinese wine started in 1892. Changyu's cute unicorn mascot, Qiqi, appeared and invited them on a magical journey flying over China to visit the company's chateaux. And thanks to 4-D, we got to go along. We felt flapping on our legs as they walked through vineyards, got splashed with droplets of water as we followed them jumping into a cauldron of wine at the next stop, and got startled by things poking us in the back for more 4-D effect. At the end, they got married at the chateau, with Changyu wine flowing for all the guests.

On the way out, the all-ages crowed couldn't stop smiling and laughing. At that point, we thought, it would be time to head to the gift shop and say goodbye. But then we were invited to board a six-seat wagon. We rolled through a haunted house train ride filled with Changyu promotion as figures of the founder, Zhang Bishi, appeared in the dark to tell the brand's story in a thunderous voice. Just, wow. But there was more. Next, we took seats at the "Dream Wine University" to watch a live theater

Dreaming of Italy at Chateau Changyu Reina.

piece with special effects. Actors appeared out of tornados, and little Qiqi (the unicorn mascot) beamed in to be quizzed about appropriate food and wine matching. We couldn't make this stuff up. Well, after all that, and a tasting, it was finally time for the gift shop. Qiqi remains the only stuffed animal Pierre has ever purchased for himself, with a Qiqi T-shirt to match.

Changyu Reina was just one (though a big one, for sure) of several wineries in the Xi'an area. This meant local employment and internship opportunities for Yangling students, on both the winemaking and the business side. In addition to the Italian castle, there was another, much quieter wine tourism spot, an hour out of the city: Jade Valley Winery and Resort, owned by Professor Ma Qingyun, a famous Chinese architect

Families playing at Chateau Changyu Reina.

and dean of the School of Architecture at the University of Southern California. After his father retired from a factory job in Xi'an and decided to spend more time in Yushan, his native village, Ma designed and built a house for him there. Over the years, Professor Ma became concerned about China's path for rural economic development, which he thought took after "bad urbanism," threatening agricultural landscapes and devaluing local labor traditions and skills. Ma's book, *C.A.N.: A Project of Agri-Urbanism*, details his approach, advocating smarter urban design to value rural land and agriculture rather than replace them.

Jade Valley was the first experiment with this model, with wine as the framework. The idea was to use wine as a vehicle to combine culture, agriculture, and nature (C.A.N. as he called it). Following the style of his father's house, he built several guesthouses, along with a winery and a room serving as visitor center and dining room. Visitors could pay for a simple tour and tasting, but also for food, and they could even spend the night at one of the resort houses, made of local stones and designed in the traditional courtyard style. Despite their creative architecture, they blended in the village landscape and offered comfortable spaces and modern bathrooms. One of the houses was a ten-minute drive from the winery, facing the vineyard and boasting a swimming pool.

We understand that many of you will never visit the college of enology. But if you ever find yourself in Xi'an to visit the famous Terracotta Warriors, now you know that wine tourism for the whole family is a short drive away. For now, our spring break is over, and it's time to stop by another wine school, back in Beijing.

* * *

We have yet to find time to get to the Terracotta Warriors. But we did walk the Great Wall. We were in the neighborhood because of wine. In July 2014, the wine world converged at a big wine exhibition nearby, in Yanqing. We found a beautiful courtyard guesthouse in Badaling, a short walk from the main entrance to the wall and a short drive from the expo. Everyone seemed tired at the end of day 1, having spent hours talking, tasting, and trading business cards. In the university corner, four women in their early twenties were still holding the fort. They were graduate students from the viticulture and enology program at China Agricultural University, another source of Chinese winemakers, marketers, and wine scientists. They poured samples of Cynthia's new favorite grape variety, Marselan, one that the program's graduate students helped to make. We loved their wine brand: *Xueyuanpai*, a word that can be translated as "the Academy" but also refers to the contrast between an armchair erudite and a practitioner. This seems like a perfect term to convey the combination of science and artful practice that winemakers need.

The Xueyuanpai wine series was part of a research project led by Professor Huang Weidong, the director of China Agricultural University's Center of Wine Science and Technology. With his students, Professor Huang worked with wineries in Xinjiang, Ningxia, Inner Mongolia, and of course, close to home in Beijing and Hebei. The idea was to explore China's terroir, figuring out what each region's sense of place means for its wines. At each location, the professor and his students made Xueyuanpai wine, and they also helped the partner wineries improve their own wines. This was a win-win for both sides, and potentially an even bigger win for the industry as a whole in the future. Being professors, we loved the idea of students being at the forefront of the ongoing pursuit to understand the terroirs of China. We also loved the wines the students poured for us at their little booth, and apparently, we were not alone. Recent vintages of Xueyuanpai won international medals at competitions in Berlin and Brussels. The following year, we visited their school, thanks to another connection from that Understanding Jiu conference at UC Davis.

People were gearing up for midautumn festival when we guest-lectured at the Department of Viticulture and Enology, where the students who made Xueyuanpai wine came from. Every shop in Beijing, including Starbucks, seemed to advertise mooncakes. Professor Lu Jiang brought tasty ones as desserts for our lunch on the high floor of a hotel near China Agricultural University's College of Food Science and Nutritional Engineering, the broader umbrella that includes the wine program. In the entrance of the building, we couldn't miss the ad for COFCO, China's giant food-processing group, which provided some funding. A grape genetics expert, Professor Lu spent many years as a professor in Florida before moving back to Beijing. Walking the hallways to his office, the labs, the beakers, and the research posters reminded us of our visit at UC Davis. The program was more research-oriented and less hands-on for winemaking than in Yangling. We saw a handful of fermentation tanks and a tiny barrel room, but they were for faculty research projects. Some students were involved, of course, but most of the practicum happened outside, in internships.

Not all wine schools, even outside of China, were blessed with the kind of training equipment or vineyards right outside the classrooms that we saw at Yangling or UC Davis. But of course, Ningxia had begun to develop its own local wine programs. And this being the country's leading wine region, there would be no shortage of vineyards or local internships.

* * *

As we walked by the vineyard of Ningxia University's Wine School, a student came out of the school vineyard to greet us. She looked at her teacher with an embarrassed smile and eyes betraying a wish she'd had more time to prepare for this unexpected challenge. Her teacher, Wang Jue, had called her over for a quick vineyard break to practice her French with Pierre. "Bonjour!" She was shy at first, but her French quickly began to come out as she talked about her studies and explained her task of the afternoon, pruning the vines. She learned and practiced all the French she knew a few steps away from these vines, in the classrooms of the Wine School of Ningxia University, for less than two years. Her dream was to go study in France.

A few minutes later, Jue called another student, this time to practice his English. He was even more shy than his French-speaking classmate but ready for his study abroad in the US the following year. For enology students, the Ningxia cohorts had wicked language skills. Earlier, Pierre had given a guest lecture on wine economics in English to twenty or so of the wine school's students, and comments often flew either in English or French, even after our assistant had translated. Clearly, the school took language study very seriously.

Ningxia University already had graduate students in viticulture and enology, but this four-year undergraduate Wine School had only opened in May 2013. By the time the first class of one hundred students graduated in spring 2017, the program had ballooned to five hundred. Many eyes were on Ningxia as China's most promising wine region, but most of the country's wine professionals came out of Yangling. So, it made sense that the local university took on the task of training the next generation of professionals.

Whether they chose winemaking, wine culture, or tourism as their specialty, all students at the Ningxia University Wine School learned about wine from the ground up. They all worked in the vineyard and learned to drive a truck. Right next to the school vineyard, construction workers were putting the finishing touches on the teaching winery building, where, as in Yangling, students would practice making wine from the grapes they grew. And with campus located on the west side of Yinchuan, the top wineries along the Helan Mountain wine route were within easy reach.

Elegant and bubbly, Jue was one of five French teachers at the Wine School. Her courses focused on oral communication, from beginner to advanced. Born in Ningxia, she fell in love with the French language during her marketing degree studies in Tianjin and started studying it on her own. She went on to spend two years in Paris and moved to Amiens for a two-year graduate degree in cultural heritage management. "Behind the language, there is always culture," Jue explained, adding that she always brought French culture into the classroom.

Whether she talks about the wine school, France, local wedding traditions, monuments, or the development of relationships between Ningxia and Arab countries, Jue's conversation was delightful and focused, and she was a genuine cultural ambassador. She was impressed with her students' creativity in group performances for their final exam. One group played a scene from *Romeo and Juliet*, some sang, and others played their own French renditions of classical Chinese theater.

Yes, it was a wine school, but students had to pick a French- or English-language training track. All this made for long class days. The Ningxia Wine School tackled the language barrier problem head on. The focus on developing students' fluency was remarkable, going well beyond a token foreign language requirement. Learning French or English was built in as a core part of the wine curriculum. The young woman we met in the school vineyard had been taking ten hours of French class per week. A few months later, she went to live her dream, studying abroad in France. She spent her first year focusing on improving her language skills in one city, before enrolling in a French university's wine program. By 2016, thirty of the five hundred students enrolled were already studying in France, with another twenty in the United States. Without the strong language training offered by teachers like Jue, this would not be possible.

By contributing research and training skilled workers, universities play a key role in the development of industries around the world. Chinese wine is no exception.

7

SUPERPOWERED GRAPES AND SUPERHERO WINEMAKERS

Liao started our visit to Guanlan Vineyard with a stop on "Rock Mountain," an aptly named pile of rocks that they'd extracted from the soil when the vineyard was planted. He had a video on his phone as a souvenir of the time when the truck was shoveling rocks out of the ground. Just watching the tiny iPhone screen, we felt how tedious the operation must have been. In the winter, we knew the landscape would be nothing but rows of rocks and dirt covering the protected vines underground. Every year, the costly fall-burying deadline weighs heavily on the mind of winemakers in Ningxia and much of China's Northwest. *Vitis vinifera*, the European grape species that brings most of the world's wine, can't handle the brutal winters of northwest China. But Liao wanted to show us that a little help from science might be on the way. Could new grapes, with superpowers that can handle the climate, provide some kind of insurance policy?

It's not a uniquely Chinese problem, by the way. Just head to Minnesota for your next wine vacation. The idea of wine from Minnesota seems to surprise people even more than Chinese wine. Winters are rough in the Midwest, consistently reaching vine-killing temperatures. So local winemakers know about burying for winter protection. Of course, labor there is not as cheap as in China, so there wouldn't be much of a viable Minnesotan wine industry if it weren't for new grape varieties with superpowers developed by researchers at the University of Minnesota. Marquette, Frontenac, or Itasca may not yet be household names for wine grape varieties, but their ability to survive the state's winter has allowed an otherwise implausible local wine industry to grow. Of course, there's still a long way to go for Minnesotan wine to get shelf space at our local supermarket. But if promising cold-hardy wine grapes are possible there (and in Iowa, Michigan . . .), maybe, just maybe, Ningxia winemakers won't have to bury entire vineyards before winter forever.

We got back in the car, and Liao drove away from Guanlan, back toward the Xixia district, the westernmost neighborhood of Yinchuan on the way to the Helan Mountain wine route. Our next stop was a farm, but one fenced all around and with security gates to get in. The farm belonged to Ningxia Nongken, the state-owned enterprise leading much of the effort to develop land for wine. There were about ten hectares of grapevines, but more than ten more were devoted to other plants, including goji berries. Once inside, Liao stopped in front of a nondescript office building and pulled out his phone to notify our host that we'd arrived. A young bespectacled woman in cuffed jeans, boots, and a black Mickey Mouse T-shirt ran out and jumped in the car. Demi worked in Beijing, but she'd been sent here for a seven-month assignment by her employer, the Chinese Academy of Sciences. Nongken partnered with the academy to use this farm for research, including a project to explore the most suitable grape varieties for the region. A couple of months earlier, Liao had attended a tasting of experimental wines made from grapes that could withstand Ningxia's brutal winter. And here we were, standing among a few rows of grapevines that, if proven successful, could save local wineries a lot of trouble and money.

"She is the king of the vineyard," Liao said, explaining that Demi was one of those rare Chinese wine graduates whose idea of a good time was hanging out in the vines. During her undergraduate years studying ecology in Beijing, she especially loved the field trips, the outdoors, and any opportunities to get her hands dirty working with plants. Her first job was with the viticulture department of the Chinese Academy of Sciences, and that's when she got interested in grapes and wine. She wanted a well-rounded understanding of the industry, so she did a vintage at a winery in Inner Mongolia and then took a wine business job in Shanghai. After two years in Adelaide to complete a master's in viticulture and enology, she went back to work where she could be outdoors, in the vines, with the academy, unlike most of her Chinese classmates, who looked for sales and marketing jobs in a big city. She mimed the hunchback posture of sitting at a desk, along with a handwriting motion, to show how boring being in an office could be.

In Ningxia's vineyards, the vines were usually planted for easy burial, so most trunks grew at an angle, closer to the ground rather than standing upright. But walking in this research vineyard with Demi and Liao, we immediately noticed something different: trunks were up, as in Shandong vineyards, where mild winters meant no burying. Indeed, these two varieties, Beimei and Beihong, survive through the winter, as do the hybrids that support the Minnesotan wine industry. Demi showed us how to tell the two apart: the little pink spot in the middle of Beimei leaves was absent from Beihong leaves. These grapes were hardly newfangled inventions. In the 1950s, Beijing researchers crossed a cold-hardy species found in northern China, *Vitis amurensis*, with a *vinifera* variety, Muscat of Hamburg. Beihong and Beimei are just two of several offspring from this unlikely marriage.

We tasted some grapes. "It's like biting into a lemon," Demi said. Liao remembered a tasting with local winemakers. The wines had good color, but the acidity was too high. So for these varieties to make commercially appealing wine, there was still a lot of work to do. Liao saw potential for blending, and Demi suggested they could be suitable for sparkling and rosé. We had fond memories of another hybrid offspring. Gérard Colin made a very good red wine from Beichun, another one in the series of the Chinese Academy's *amurensis* crossings from the early 1950s. Gérard liked to make wine he couldn't make just anywhere, and the one we tasted with him at Puchang in Xinjiang was exciting indeed. Pierre once tasted a Beihong dry red at a Ningxia wine conference. "It's a love it or hate it wine," a famous Ningxia winemaker told him. Good wine from winter-resistant grapevines may be possible after all, but people have to be convinced to buy it. It can be done. After all, Vermont winemakers like Deirdre Heekin of La Garagista or Krista Scruggs of Zafa Wines have been getting attention for their wines from hybrid grapes. Why not China?

A short drive up on the farm, across the path from sunflowers and a minute away from an unusually loud, densely populated army of ducks, there were also more familiar grapes, such as Chardonnay, Riesling, and Cabernet Sauvignon. We learned that the Nongken farm was only one part of Beijing scientists' grape research. In Ningxia, the academy worked on ten different vineyard sites. By selling grapes to local wineries and following up on the results, researchers explored where different varieties fared best. This made sense, and it seemed like the kind of research any emerging wine region would do to invest in future development. We left hopeful for the future of Chinese wine, and we speculated about what research might have attracted the duck army. Meanwhile, back at the college of enology near Xi'an, graduate students played with other superpowered grapes.

* * *

Summer and her classmate washed a couple of glasses and filled them from the tap on tank number two. The students, both starting year 2 of their master's degree at Li Hua's College of Enology, were nervous but excited to show us their research at a local winery, a short drive away from campus. We couldn't wait to taste their wine project, Ecolly (pronounced "ee-ko-lee," a sound translation for the Chinese name of a local white grape in Yangling). The sun was out during our student-led tour in September, but puddles punctuated the ground, a reminder of heavy rains earlier that week. The students told us that summer rain was the toughest part of the work here. Humid weather right during prime growing season could leave grapes vulnerable to rot. Imagine students' nightmares before the fall semester starts: will there be enough healthy grapes left to practice? Yangling students were learning viticulture the hard way. It helped that in the 1990s, Li Hua and his colleagues had bred two varieties, the white Ecolly, and the red Meili, for their resistance to disease. Our young expert guides planned to get the most insight out of their Ecolly tank by using half for a dry white wine and distilling the rest into brandy. A few feet away, the winery's own wines were also fermenting in tanks marked with large blue Chinese characters: Li Hua Brand. In exchange for using Professor Li's fame as the brand, the winery offered space for students to practice, and the faculty used part of the vineyard in their research to find the best grape varieties for Shaanxi.

As promising as superpowered grapes may be from the perspective of a viticulture scientist, their marketability is a challenge. Wines made from hybrid varieties sometimes taste different from what wine drinkers expect. Maybe winemakers will find a way to make wines with broad appeal from them, or maybe it will remain a small niche. But in the meantime, so much can be learned. Researchers continue their quest for local solutions to local problems, and students practice their chops. We enjoyed Li Hua's Meili rosé during yet another wonderful foodie dinner with Professor Li Jiagui in Yangling, at an unassuming restaurant serving Xinjiang cuisine. Standing next to the big plate of lamb and noodles on the table, a young Li Hua in a cap and gown, painted on both bottle and cork, set the perfect tone for us to eat, drink, and learn. Our next stop will take us beyond the confines of universities and science labs, where superhero winemaking consultants help shape the future of Chinese wine.

* * *

"On to the red Bordeaux varietals over ten pounds. And the winner is . . . the 2009 from Helan Qingxue!" This was the announcement that stunned the wine world at the 2011 Decanter World Wine Awards. The winery's chairman, Rong Jian, was there to collect the award. He got on stage to shake hands and take pictures with wine celebrity Steven Spurrier, the one who had organized the famous 1976 Judgment of Paris, where California wines topped the best Bordeaux and Burgundies at a blind tasting with French judges. Helan Qingxue's winemaker, Zhang Jing, wasn't there, but her famous consultant, Li Demei, made the trip and spoke to the camera in English after the ceremony: "It's a surprise, so, I never think we can win this so high, highest trophy. I'm very excited."[1] An associate professor of wine tasting and enology at Beijing Agriculture College, Li holds a master's degree in fruit tree science and an interdisciplinary engineering degree from Bordeaux combining viticulture, enology, and economics. In addition to Helan Qingxue, he consults for several other wineries in Ningxia and Xinjiang. "Demei's View," his regular, always insightful column for *Decanter China* magazine, covers a wide range of topics, from vineyard field reports, commentary on China's wine market, and wine marketing to natural wine and the prospects for various grape varieties. So, Professor Li is a Chinese wine superhero in many ways, as not just a winemaker but also an influential writer.

Several people we met more recently referred to his March 2017 column, "Marselan: The Future 'Signature' of China." We'd had a soft spot for Marselan ever since that Grace Vineyard barrel tasting during our first week in China. The more we saw, the more those experimental tastings felt like history in the making. With so much Cabernet Sauvignon in China, presumably due to Bordeaux envy in the early days, it's refreshing to see wineries experimenting. Professor Li's article drew attention to the fact that several wineries in different parts of China had been experimenting with Marselan with good success.

Have you ever had Marselan? This southern French grape variety, a crossing between Cabernet Sauvignon and Grenache, was invented in a lab, in 1961, by French researcher Paul Truel. It's sometimes found in red blends from the Languedoc region but is rarely highlighted as the star of any show. So, you won't just run into it at a shop the way you would with Merlot or Syrah. And yet, there are examples from all around the world. We found one in a little Seattle wine shop, thanks to encouragement from Jim Boyce, the innovative wine blogger behind the *Grape Wall of China* blog who launched the first World Marselan Day. The inaugural 2018 #worldmarselanday happened on April 27, Paul Truel's birthday.

This is a pretty big departure from Cabernet Gernischt, a widely planted red grape that Changyu first marketed in 1937.[2] Changyu also has a World Cabernet Gernischt Day (May 25), which seemed to have brand potential because the grape makes good wine and it's unique to China. But what is Cabernet Gernischt exactly? Geneticists recently found that what they studied was actually Carmenere (Chile's signature grape). Others suggest some vines are actually Cabernet Franc, and some think the name comes from nineteenth-century vines imported with a German label, "Cabernet gemischt" (meaning simply "mixed Cabernet").[3] We're happy with any wine that tastes good, but we can see how there may be less marketing potential for a celebration around "World 'might be one of several things with one convenient label' Day."

You may be more familiar with World Malbec Day, celebrated every year on April 17 (and if you weren't, now you can look forward to a great last couple of weeks of April next year). This one was invented in 2011, by Wines of Argentina, the trade body that promotes the country's wines. Malbec is now everywhere, and we must thank Argentina for making the grape, originally from France, so popular worldwide. Malbec drove the Argentinean wine revival through the 1990s and early 2000s. There's even a movie about it: *Boom Varietal*.

Malbec is Argentina's "signature grape variety," and you may know others, such as Oregon Pinot Noir and New Zealand Sauvignon Blanc, that have made New World wine regions successful. Check those aisles at any grocery store's wine department, and you'll see what Professor Li meant by "signature grape variety." Marselan may be unknown, but it is a tried and tested grape variety that can make deep-colored, delicious, approachable red wines, of the kind many people know and love. Unlike special hybrids like Meili or Beihong, farmers will have to bury it every winter. But if we believe Professor Li's argument, maybe Marselan has a different kind of superpower: to put China on the world wine map for rehabilitating a grape most people forgot about. Next, we're off to meet another winemaking superhero, less known outside of China but no less super.

* * *

Checking on the bottle labels and cases packed for shipping, cracking jokes while tasting in a small group, showing off the latest finished rooms, and figuring out where to hang a large painting, Crazy Fang was in intense multitasking mode as she paced around her winery. More good things had happened since our first visit to Kanaan winery a year earlier. A major distributor, Summergate, recently acquired by the Australian Woolworths Liquor Group as a small step into the Chinese market, took Kanaan wines under its wing, as the only Chinese wine in their portfolio. For Kanaan, Summergate's broad reach, thanks to thirteen offices across the country, meant more placements in high-end restaurants and hotels, and the occasional busy schedule of winemaker dinner tours in big cities. Kanaan is one of those successes that combines good quality, competitive prices, and clever marketing around Fang's charisma and her obsession with horses. Remember, Fang had no professional wine background before her dad convinced her to come home from Germany and invest in Ningxia. The fast rise of Kanaan certainly confirmed her reputation as a notoriously fast learner and talented taster. But like many winemaking newbies around the world, she also had a secret weapon: Zhou Shuzhen, a small-framed woman with a kind but serious face. In fact, that day, we didn't know we were going to Kanaan at all. We were honored to be shadowing Zhou Laoshi (Professor Zhou) for a day, and when we landed at Kanaan, we realized Fang was one of her clients.

When Zhou Shuzhen went to college, shortly after Deng Xiaoping started opening China to the rest of the world, there was no such thing as a wine major. She studied economics. But after graduation, she got interested in wine and worked under Guo Qichang, a pioneer of Chinese wine research you rarely hear about in English but who played a very important role early on. According to one source, Professor Guo's involvement in wine came from a dramatic event. A leak at a chemical plant where he worked as a chemical engineer had left him seriously injured. It was during his recovery back home that he was invited to work for the Qingdao (aka Tsingtao) brewery in Shandong, back in the late 1940s.[4] One thing led to another, and over the next three decades, he would be at the forefront of research into the best grape varieties for Chinese wine, at a time when local grapes were widely used. Professor Guo became one of the leading voices recommending that Chinese wineries focus instead on grape varieties of the European *Vitis vinifera* species exclusively.[5]

Working under Guo on early experiments with modern dry red wine made of Cabernet Sauvignon in 1983, Professor Zhou developed her wine chops at a time when few people cared, and the sector was even more dominated by men than it is today. After years of moving up the ranks, acquiring certifications as a wine judge and then winemaker, she worked for Ningxia's giant Xixia King winery, and then joined the winemaking team at Helan Mountain winery even before Pernod Ricard purchased the place. Then, in the summer of 2014, she decided to become her own boss and offer her services as a consultant, or "independent winemaker." When you think about experts and consultants in Chinese wine, it's tempting to picture foreigners, like Gérard Colin, coming to the rescue, or foreign-trained Chinese experts who speak English and French, like Li Demei. Their foreign credentials give them an aura of authority and cachet. Professor Zhou, who didn't study abroad, and doesn't speak English or French, may not have Li's global fame, but her contribution to Ningxia wine, and local fame, are no less important.

There are more Chinese independent winemakers, largely unknown to the public. Early on at a big banquet for a state-owned Ningxia winery, we met a winemaker who loved his work but told us he missed his family on the coast. Two years later, we ran into him at a conference and learned that he, too, had adopted the independent winemaker lifestyle, perhaps because it gave him more freedom.

Wine consultants, sometimes called "flying winemakers," have been a major force in the wine world for a long time. Californian Paul Hobbs is credited as one of the leaders (working with locals like Nicolas Catena) of the modernization of Argentine wine. In the United States, Andre Tchelistcheff, a Russian who studied winemaking in France, known as "California's most influential winemaker since the repeal of Prohibition,"[6] spent the last two decades of his career consulting not only in California but also in Washington, notably with Chateau Ste Michelle. In China,

COFCO (which owns Great Wall wine) snapped an exclusive deal with Michel Rolland, perhaps the most famous flying winemaker in the world. Rolland, who consults with several of the top wineries in Napa, has something like two hundred clients around the world. His name is even on a few Grover Zampa wines, from India. In emerging wine regions, flying winemakers help spread technical skill and raise the level of all wines. But at the same time, their detractors argue, their influence could be so strong that all the wines they make, no matter where they are, tend to converge. You'll find people on both sides of this debate. A Chinese wine marketer once told us that she found many Ningxia wines a bit too similar and speculated that maybe it was because Professors Zhou and Li left their mark in several of the best wines. True or not, at this early stage of development, some level of homogenization seemed like a small price to pay for a significant bump in quality.

"I just want to hang out and drink," Crazy Fang said. She told us she didn't like formal wine tastings, adding that she's not a professional winemaker. "She [Zhou] is a pro, but she's a nice woman." When Fang started, her father, one of Jiabeilan's founders, knew Professor Zhou and recommended her as Kanaan's winemaker. Professor Zhou told us it was convenient that she had four clients located in the same area. During harvest time, she visited each winemaker every day, transitioning to every other day through the fermentation process. She worked closely with each winery's in-house winemaking team. She explained that one of the best things about her job was how the variety of grapes from different clients allowed her to vary her winemaking decisions.

Before our visit to Kanaan, Professor Zhou had taken us to another client, Legacy Peak winery. The owner, Liu Hai, started the winery in 2010, but his father had planted the vineyard in 1997 so that the family could sell grapes to wineries. The rare eighteen-year-old vines were a serious asset in Ningxia. When we visited, Legacy Peak was already one of Ningxia's success stories, in terms of both quality and sales. They were among three Chinese wineries on the portfolio of East Meets West (EMW), a distributor otherwise specialized in imports. The Peninsula Hotel bought three thousand bottles a year, Liu Hai said. Combined with Kanaan's deal at competing distributor Summergate, we were giddy with the idea that they would show up in hotels where wine enthusiasts might find them.

Despite what one might think of the influence of consultants, we found that the wine styles varied quite a bit, not just between Kanaan and Legacy Peak but also within each winery. Above all, Professor Zhou wanted to make fresh, lively wines. "Some say tannins are the soul of red wine, but acidity is important," she explained. Keeping that freshness, preventing the wines from being heavy, was one of her guiding principles. But we were also struck by her attention to consumer tastes, something she told us she discussed at length with each client. EMW regularly sent a rep to taste Legacy Peak wines to report on how they perceived any evolution in consumer preferences. Zhou also had strong views on appropriate pricing, something she said distributors like EMW and Summergate did well. Another Ningxia winery, she explained, once charged three different prices to three members of the same family. "They're inexperienced with the politics of price," she said.

The more we learned about homegrown wine programs and scientific research, as well as superhero winemakers like Professor Zhou, the more we bristled at the notion that good Chinese wine depended on foreign

Professor Zhou explains key strategies in the vineyard at Legacy Peak.

experts. An already large, and growing, crew of Chinese winemakers and scientists are making a difference. Still, for a young wine region like Ningxia, Professor Zhou told us that it was important to learn from foreign winemakers. At the same time, she pointed out that foreigners needed to learn about the local climate and soils from their Chinese colleagues. The Ningxia government designed a promotional event to promote just that kind of exchange, in the form of a friendly winemaking competition. In fact, you've already met one of the participants, a curious, energetic Italian, back when she taught at Li Hua's college of enology.

* * *

Do you remember Denise, from "the perfect couple"? She used to teach wine culture at the college of enology in Yangling. If students there fell in love with Italian wine, that was thanks to Denise and her partner Alessio. In 2015, while still lecturers in Yangling, Denise and Alessio took part in the second edition of the Ningxia Winemaker's Challenge, a contest organized by Ningxia wine authorities. The inaugural challenge, in 2012, began with just seven winemakers, each from a different country. But in her cohort, Denise was among forty-eight competitors from seventeen different countries. At the ceremony launching the contest, each contestant was randomly matched with a winery and three hectares of vines. Serious business started with supervising the harvest. Then they had two years to visit regularly and, working with the winery's staff, produce a special bottling for the competition. Finally, the wines were judged by a panel composed of prominent foreign and Chinese wine experts, who awarded medals based on a blind tasting.

Although she didn't win, Denise was happy about this first experience working in Ningxia. She was matched with one of our early Ningxia loves, Leirenshou, and had fun discovering the unique way grapevines were planted and how to navigate cultural differences. During her visits, she stayed at the winery, making fond memories of times when the owner's skilled-interpreter daughter wasn't available, leaving her and the staff using "a lot of body language and laughing." There was really nothing like the Ningxia Winemaker's Challenge anywhere else in the wine world, so she was excited to be part of this unique experience.

Like other contestants, she made a total of five thousand bottles, including three thousand for the government wine bureau. The bureau sold its share of contestant bottles with a 2015 Ningxia Winemaker's Challenge label on Jingdong, an e-commerce platform. The set price, over which competitors had no say, was around 400 yuan for gold medalist bottles, 228 for silver, and 128 for the rest. Denise regretted not being able to influence the price, as she thought she would have been able to sell her two thousand bottles for a bit more. She also wished she could have experimented beyond Cabernet Sauvignon. But in the end, she did sell all two thousand bottles and overall loved the opportunity.

The challenge sounded like a win-win. Foreign and local winemakers learned a lot from each other, and everyone got some publicity, courtesy of the local government. Plus, foreign contestants could even make a little money from selling their two thousand bottles. Though on that last part, not everyone could do what Denise and Alessio did. We have always envied people with Chinese bank accounts, able to buy and sell whatever they need with the click of a button, and we assumed that gave the perfect couple an advantage in selling their wines. But even that wasn't necessary. When we asked how they were able to sell all of their bottles without labels or packaging, Denise replied, "One word. I'll give you the answer in one word: *guanxi*."

It was hard to imagine the other several dozen winemakers following in those footsteps, selling their wines by relying on extensive social networks in the country where Denise and Alessio had lived and worked for several years. Imagine being one of the winemakers who had to fly in internationally every time a visit to the winery was needed. Now picture your wine, which you are supposed to sell yourself, held at a warehouse in Ningxia. Sure, you can pack a few bottles in your checked luggage, but how would you go about selling your wine in China? And to whom? In theory, you can get some samples sent to your country, but beware of serious delays and fees to get them through customs. What's more, apparently the wines would only be held at the facility for one year. After that, well, who knows what will happen?

"It was equal parts awesome and frustrating," said Mike Gadd, an Australian contestant from Margaret River, in an interview with his hometown's newspaper.[7] While he, like Denise, got a good winery and vineyard block draw, not everybody was as happy, he reported. Participants complained about lacking resources, the lack of government responsiveness to their requests for help, and the fact that much of the quality of their future wine could be determined by the random draw. As if this wasn't enough, it turns out that the bureau only planned to buy labels and capsules for their own three thousand bottles. So, a winemaker seeking to sell their two thousand bottles would have to do this themselves.

Well, there must be rules for the competition, and after all, this is primarily a big publicity stunt for the region. It seemed healthy to approach the challenge as Denise did, as an opportunity for learning, cultural exchange, and the rush of taking part in something truly unique.

We asked how long the perfect couple planned to continue working in China and how they managed travel and visas. Although they were happy with their work, she expected that they would eventually have to leave China. "Being a foreigner in a foreign country is not easy, even from a legal point of view." She described visa nightmares, grateful that the winery she now worked for in Shandong, Chateau Nine Peaks, had taken care of her immigration paperwork. This isn't just annoying for the foreigner, she explained. It's hard to imagine most companies going through all that effort when there are more and more skilled Chinese winemakers every year. For a long time, there was only one college. Then, suddenly, there were five. Many of those students go on to complete graduate degrees abroad before returning home. Plus, now that there are so many places making good wine in China, students who can't travel abroad can still hone their skills in diverse wine regions and different environments. There's more than one way to work in a foreign land, and many of them are still in China.

8

THE MOUNTAIN GUIDE

"**S**imply complete your contact details below and we'll get back to you shortly." Cynthia rolled her eyes as Pierre complied with the instructions on Moët Hennessy Estates's website, hoping we could get invited to visit their new winery in Yunnan Province. Predictably, we never heard back. A more personal contact through a friend didn't help either. At the time, we'd only heard of two high-profile wine writers visiting this major foreign venture into the Chinese wine industry: Jancis Robinson and Jane Anson. Having failed through official channels, Pierre was ready to give up on the northwestern Yunnan trip altogether. To him, it seemed like a long and expensive journey to the middle of nowhere, with no guarantee we would talk to a single person in the wine industry. But Cynthia put her foot down: "Oh, we're going anyway." She was right of course. It turned out there was much more to local wine than an official interview at Moët.

* * *

With its comfy chairs, fireplace, friendly dog, and Bob Marley tunes, our first bar in Shangri-la wasn't without a hipster vibe. It was one of many bars in the tourist part of town that advertised local wine at the front door. In August 2015, with the harvest coming up, most of that year's wines from villages in nearby Deqin County were long sold out and consumed, but our bar had one ice wine available. You might know ice wine from Germany, Austria, or Canada, where grapes are on the vine well into the fall, waiting for the first hard cold to freeze them on the spot. Grape pickers are urgently summoned to harvest the frozen berries. When pressed, the ice crystals are separated, leaving behind highly concentrated juice loaded with sugar and balancing acidity, the base to make luscious sweet wines. The barman told us that this one was different though, with grapes frozen after picking. This is what some wine pros call icebox wine, with a certain disdain. But we were impressed. Until then, we had only tasted homemade wine in regions where farmers struggle to ripen grapes fully. Here, the sweet wine was dark and rich, and its texture reminded us of a port. It went perfectly with our yak jerky appetizer.

The fact that today Shangri-la is a world-renowned tourist destination is a testament to what clever promotion and targeted government subsidies can achieve. Just twenty years ago, few people knew about this little part of the Diqing Tibetan Autonomous Prefecture. The county wasn't even called Shangri-la but Zhongdian. Back in the 1980s, locals depended on subsistence farming, largely cut off from the rest of the world by impassable mountains. Since their livelihoods didn't provide much tax revenue, the government took advantage of rich forest resources to invest in timber. The economy became so dependent on timber that at one point, the sector made up over 80 percent of local GDP. But in 1998, after floods killed thousands and displaced millions in several provinces, China's central government, concerned about the consequences of deforestation, banned commercial logging. The main source of Diqing government money vanished. Fortunately, by then, the authorities, seeing the end of timber coming, had already turned their attention to tourism for economic development. That's when place branding came to do its magic, helped by grants from the national government.

People knew that it was a site somewhere in the area that inspired Shangri-la, the mythical destination of James Hilton's 1933 novel, *Lost Horizon*, turned Hollywood blockbuster by Frank Capra a few years later. In the story, four Brits and an American survive a plane crash somewhere in the Himalayas and find themselves in a magical place where Buddhists and Christians live in harmony. That was a great story to attract tourists, but where exactly was the real Shangri-la? Nobody could tell, since, you know, it didn't exist. So, in the mid-1990s, local authorities commissioned a surprisingly thorough interdisciplinary research project to find the "real" Shangri-la. Several sites competed for the title, but Diqing looked as if it fit the part: the rivers lined up with the story, and apparently an American plane even crashed in Zhongdian at some point. Problem

Handprinted sign advertising wine in Shangri-la.

solved. In 2001, Zhongdian was officially renamed Shangri-la, just in time for traffic to pick up at the first-ever local airport, opened in 1999.

It worked. Tourism boomed, and GDP soared. In what used to be an isolated logging village, today you can find hotel and restaurant reviews in multiple languages on the internet. At just over 6,500 feet, the elevation is high enough for surprising bursts of cold in August, just enough for airport vendors to sell expensive fleece clothing. Shangri-la is known as the last outpost before Tibet, and the path over the mountains to the Tibet Autonomous Region includes must-see destinations for many foreign and Chinese travelers.

The city of Shangri-la has a modern side with unremarkable concrete buildings. The fun for tourists happens in a specific ancient part of the city with a 1,300-year history, the Dukezhong neighborhood. It feels simultaneously ancient and new, and much of the city is very new indeed. Walking through the old town in August 2015, shopping for Tibetan handicrafts, we couldn't miss the evidence of a recent disaster. On a Saturday morning in January 2014, two-thirds of Dukezhong burned in a fire that took ten hours to put out. Some wooden houses still had visible burn marks, but reconstruction was well underway and the tourists were back.[1]

Even well before the tragedy, with the authorities' push to develop tourism, much was renovated or newly built following various architects' interpretations of neo-Tibetan architecture, leading to an impressive blend of commercialism and Tibetan hospitality. All over the ancient city, small shops carrying designer ski clothes are nested with Buddhist handicrafts and jewelry, as well as knit scarves and mittens that came in particularly handy since we skipped the airport sales. Most restaurants cater to visitors from China and abroad seeking local delicacies like yak hot pot and international foods made with local ingredients. How about a yak burger and then a yak cheesecake to finish? One place advertised a "menu en français," while its neighbor had a sign for the "menu in English." And don't miss a taste of local beer at the Socialism Bar.

At a tourist center by the main square, we told the attendant we wanted to see vineyards and try local wine. Did they have any organized wine tourism? Not really, she explained, but most residents in nearby Deqin County knew someone who made wine. In fact, her brother was a home winemaker. Farmers would sell most of their grapes to a large, local state-owned winery in October for its dry reds, but they kept the ripest fruit for their own wines, the kind we saw in bars and restaurants. Because of the number of tourists in the area, many farmers also operated guesthouses.

Where to go from here? Remember, we weren't invited by anyone, and our dream Yunnan wine route was not in the *Lonely Planet China*. So naturally, we turned to a wine anthropologist. Few foreigners know the local wine economy as well as our colleague Brendan Galipeau, now a postdoctoral researcher at Rice University. Unlike famous wine critics, Brendan wasn't chauffeured up the mountains with Moët Hennessy's executives for a quick promotional visit. He was still an undergraduate when he fell in love with the region and devoted the next several years as a PhD student to understanding its people and natural resources. The young, Mandarin-speaking, red-haired American must have become instantly recognizable the minute he settled in a small village for his research, living with a family, helping with harvesting fruits and walnuts, herding flocks of yaks, and socializing with locals who drink and play cards after work. Thanks to Brendan, we finally had wine plans, and we wouldn't even have to herd a single yak.

* * *

Vrooooom! Vroooom! The minivan's engine worked so hard we feared it could give out any minute, but our experienced driver didn't seem worried. Our research assistant, Joyce, then enrolled in a master's degree in translation in the coastal city of Fuzhou, had not imagined we would come all this way for wine research. Cynthia couldn't stop giggling as she popped her head in and out of the window to look down the cliff, which at times wasn't separated at all from the road. Hire a good driver, we were told. Going up the mountains away from Shangri-la, the views of vineyards in the hills were breathtaking. At one popular stop, we followed Chinese tourists' lead and took pictures in front of colorful Tibetan prayer flags and numbers painted on rocks: 4292. That's the elevation in meters, over 14,000 feet. The local mountain, Kawagarbo in Tibetan, also known by its Chinese name, Meili Xue Shan (Meili Snow Mountain), is both a major tourist attraction and a sacred Tibetan Buddhist site. The top peak stands at a whopping 22,110 feet. From the comfort of our van, we felt for those who walked or bicycled up the pilgrimage route. None of us suffered from altitude sickness, despite many warnings we heard, though Cynthia experienced just enough oxygen deprivation to make looking down the cliff especially thrilling.

Cizhong, one of the villages Brendan recommended, feels like the middle of nowhere. From Shangri-la (the nearest airport), it takes a five-to eight-hour drive, depending on the weather. To access the village from the main road, you first cross a noisy and shaky bridge above the river, and the one-car-at-a-time rule seems appropriate. And yet, the village is featured in many English-language travel guides. We landed there following the wine, but that's not why tourists come to Cizhong. They want to see the Catholic church, a remnant from the work of French and Swiss missionaries a century ago. Many villagers are practicing Catholics, attend mass every Sunday, and celebrate holidays. When you have a moment, do a little online research for Cizhong. You'll find not only the village on Google Maps but also the church itself, online reviews on Trip Advisor, and a YouTube video of mass. Somehow, visiting Tibetan Catholic communities has become one of the cool things to do in the region.[2] And of course, the church has its own vineyard, since French and Swiss priests needed a source to make sacramental wine.

Cizhong may not look like your typical wine vacation. It's as far (in many ways) from Napa Valley as it can be. But to take advantage of the tourism boom, many villagers operate guesthouses, grow grapes, and make wine. If you prefer an upgrade from farm living, the local Songstam chain offers luxury (and expensive) accommodation. So, yes, you can do wine tourism here. The foreign-language guidebooks may not call it that, but several online reviewers who traveled to Cizhong mention the local wine. So, we would learn, did the Mandarin version of the *Lonely Planet Yunnan*.

Past our beautiful but shaky bridge into the village, our driver had to stop and let us finish on foot, rolling our wine suitcase on scattered parts of a new road in progress. Behind us, the construction site for a new, taller, sturdier bridge was another sign of a big local infrastructure project. The new dam would raise the river high enough to flood Yanmen, a village upstream, forcing its residents to relocate to Cizhong. Cizhong itself survived, despite some fears, though villagers lost some land and we've heard it's less picturesque than when we visited. The story is a good reminder that farmers' land rights are never truly secure.

We rolled along all the way to our destination, the Rose Honey guesthouse, where Brendan spent time living and working with a Catholic family of winegrowers. While Cabernet Sauvignon is widely planted in the area, Rose Honey grapes give Cizhong wine its claim to fame. The grape variety has French origins, from the time missionaries came here and built the church. After the phylloxera blight destroyed much of France's vineyards in the late nineteenth century, Rose Honey was never replanted there. Today, Yunnan seems to be the only place in the world that has it.

Winemaker/farmer Hongxing perches atop Cizhong Cathedral overlooking the church vineyard.

In our basic but comfortable room at the Rose Honey guesthouse, a Jesus painting added a touch of color to the bare white walls. In the courtyard, a monkey sat in its cage, chickens ran around, and cows enjoyed their meal. Our host, middle-aged Hongxing, learned to make wine from his father, Wu Gongdi, a pioneer of the local wine revival and leader in the church management association. It is easy to feel out of shape when you watch old Wu Gongdi walk a heavy basket of grapes on his back out of the vineyard while casually picking up his cell phone. Back in 1998, he was the first to make wine with Rose Honey grapes from the church's vineyard. The family played a big role in making wine an important sector in Cizhong.[3]

Harvest began on the day we arrived. Once the grapes were in, Hongxing and his father led the winemaking in the courtyard, helped by everybody in the house. They used to crush grapes by hand, but Hongxing designed and built a motor-operated artisanal crusher himself. The juice ran down to a big tarp where Wu Gongdi's wife removed the stems by

Winemaker/farmer Wu Gongdi takes a call while harvesting by hand.

hand, tossing them in a separate bin. The crushed grapes then went in large plastic bins, where they would ferment for two weeks. Like all red wine, a cap forms on top as the skins move up, pushed by carbon dioxide. Three times a day, Hongxing and his family would punch the cap down using a fork-shaped wooden stick. Punch-downs are a key move in red winemaking to maximize exposure of the juice to skins, extract color and taste, and prevent spoilage on top. Finally, they transfer the juice to two stainless steel tanks and two oak barrels, through a wooden syphoning device to keep skins out of the way. The family didn't add yeast or sugar, nor did they use any pesticides, something Wu Gongdi seemed proud of as he mimed the operation of a pesticide sprayer with a disapproving look.

They sold most of the wine in plastic jugs, but some was bottled under a Cizhong wine label with a picture of the church. The part we saw was the year's first harvest, but there would be grapes coming in later to make a popular late-harvest wine. Unfortunately for us, the family had long sold out of their wines. Big buyers included bars in places as far as Lijiang and Dali, both well over a nine-hour drive away. Cizhong wine was famous enough in the region that bars like the ones we saw in Shangri-la advertised the name as a selling point. Add to that the tourist "cellar door" market, and you can see why most grape farmers in Cizhong made their own wine rather than selling grapes.

Hongxing served wine he bought from the neighbor to go with a delicious lunch prepared by his sister. We toasted with fellow tourist guests who had just come back from a visit to the church. The man, who spoke little English but introduced himself by his English name, Ian, was here on vacation with his wife and little daughter, mainly to visit the key tourist sites. But he was also a wine enthusiast, and his work as a professional photographer had taken him to Napa and Bordeaux's Chateau Lafite and Mouton Rothschild. He told us he preferred "xin shijie de jiu—New World wine," he repeated in English. They could have stayed anywhere, but Ian's interest in wine brought the family to the Rose Honey guesthouse. Had we just met a Cizhong wine tourist? You see, our *Lonely Planet* did not mention wine even in passing, but Ian's *Lonely Planet Yunnan*—the Chinese edition, of course—had a whole paragraph about Hongxing's guesthouse, with praise for the wine.

More visitors come here than you'd think at first glance. In the house guestbook, children's drawings mix with messages in Chinese, English,

Cynthia gets to help with the handmade crusher.

and French, sometimes with a Catholic tone. An experienced trekking guide, Hongxing takes guests up in the mountains to hike and spend the night at a little cottage. Still, wine sales remain the family's main source of income. Despite the upheaval caused by the dam project, Hongxing's recent (2019) WeChat posts suggest they're doing well. He opened a wine shop near the cathedral and got married. Since 2017, he's been getting advice from French winemakers who've started their own winery, Xiaoling Estate in Cigu, a nearby village. When done well, this kind of exchange of expertise is an important part of improving emerging industries. Remember how Ningxia's independent winemaker, Professor Zhou Shuzhen, explained that winemakers need to learn from each other to make the best wine. But the innovation of farmers like Hongxing goes far beyond the winemaking. With relatively few resources, they have developed a distinctive brand of tourism around culture, religion, nature, and wine. And it's not just in Cizhong.

* * *

Sitting on a patch of dirt and weeds a few feet behind a row of grapevines, much hilarity ensued between our host Zhuge and her friends as they took a break from work and shared some snacks. Our assistant, Joyce, didn't get the jokes any better than we did. Like everywhere in the region, most people speak Tibetan. Having completed only the second grade, Zhuge became fluent in Mandarin as she developed her business. A grape grower and winemaker, she interacts with tourists in Bu village, located near the popular Mingyong Glacier in Meili Snow Mountain. A local charter bus has a stop in the village, and as in Cizhong, some homes, including Zhuge's, double as guesthouses.

With rooms in her own house occupied by construction workers, Zhuge found space for us across the street at her father's. He's a bit of a local celebrity. In his day, he used sniper-like skills to shoot hundreds of wild animals. But then, there was that time he shot a black bear. As he explained in an interview with the *China Daily* newspaper, it changed everything. Every kill after that made him sick with hallucinations. Maybe he had angered the mountains' god, he thought. So, he gave up the gun and became a ranger, using his insider's knowledge of hunting to patrol with his team and fight against poaching. Thanks to people like him, a local official told the paper, hunting went down, and life improved for endangered animals.[4] Of course, there are other threats to the biodiversity of the region, like infrastructure development and tourism. The Nature Conservancy, an American environmental nonprofit, runs projects in the Meili Snow Mountain supporting local efforts to balance economic development and conservation.

The switch from poacher to conservation advocate was a noble move, but it also meant giving up meat sales, a significant source of family income. His daughter's wine business must have helped. Like many villagers in the region, Zhuge planted vines back in 2001, at the time the government promoted and subsidized wine grapes as a cash crop. Farmers were drawn to the promise of sales to the state-owned Shangri-la Wine Company, which to this day has a lock over most grape contracts in the area. If you grow grapes for the company, she explained, they even send you a mystery package of pesticides to guarantee everything goes according to plan. Since she kept her grapes for her own wines, she chose not to use pesticides.

Zhuge used to grow more things, such as apples, pears, nuts, and barley, which required more pesticides. Following the government's push for wine grapes, many farmers across the region ripped out existing crops to focus on vineyards. Anthropologist Brendan Galipeau's research in other villages shows that while wine grapes brought good money, the shift could threaten food security. People used to grow much of what they ate, but livelihoods are now very dependent on sales to the wine company. As in Cizhong, some farmers started making their own wine instead of selling grapes. It sounds like a good way to gain independence, but it doesn't solve the food question. Moreover, not everybody is as skilled at winemaking as Hongxing and Zhuge.[5]

Seated on low stools around the table in Zhuge's dimly lit kitchen, we enjoyed dinner and, thanks to Joyce, conversation. A middle-aged woman joined us. Coming all the way from a village called Adong, Xiaomei just happened to spend the night at her good friend Zhuge's house, and our chat turned to our little adventure. "Oh, her sister works with the French company," Joyce translated. That's when Pierre finally got it. You see, Moët Hennessy's winery is in Adong. Cynthia, who loves rural field research, knew what she was doing back when she booked the expensive flights to Shangri-la. Our friend Mike calls this her "commando fieldwork tactics." After dinner, Xiaomei made the call, and Zhuge helped book a Mandarin-speaking driver for the morning. Who cares if we're not VIP guests of a global luxury conglomerate? We're coming to hang out with Zhuge's friend's sister.

* * *

View of Adong village.

Holding on to whatever rocks and branches we could, ducking under fences and climbing over wires, we struggled to keep up with the old woman in flip-flops. To us, the steep path down to her vineyard felt like an obstacle course straight out of the TV show *American Ninja Warrior*. But Zhuge's friend's sister seemed fine. Yunnan's elderly grape growers really have a way of making you feel unfit. Plus, it was hard not to be distracted by the stunning views. Past patches of scattered small vineyard blocks, a Martini-glass-shaped opening between two hillsides framed the postcard-ready scenery.

Thinking we only had a couple of hours to spend here, we sat down to chat in the family dining room with our new fitness role model. Soon, a man with a big reputation as a Tibetan doctor joined the conversation. The family still grew some of its own grapes for sale to the Shangri-la Wine Company, which paid a little over five yuan per kilo on average. But like all grape farmers around, the family leased vineyard land out to Moët Hennessy. The French company settled here for its ambitious project: making a Chinese red wine that could stand next to the world's greatest.

For this, the company needed to grow the best possible grapes. More accessible wine regions, such as Ningxia and Shandong, were not deemed good enough for Moët Hennessy Louis Vuitton's ambitions. The region's low latitude meant that unlike in northern China, vines wouldn't freeze to death in the winter. The seriously high elevation (like, exploding shampoo bottle high) brought hot, bright, sunny days to help the grapes accumulate sugar and flavor, balanced with cool nights to preserve the berries' natural acidity and keep the wine fresh. And thanks to well-drained soils and evaporation so strong that bouts of summer rain dried almost instantly, Moët's winemakers had the luxury of keeping grapes on the vines disease-free well into the fall so they ripened to perfection.

To gain access to all this, Moët went into a joint venture with VATS, which, thanks to its near monopoly on the area's grapes, was happy to make a little slice available and boost the image of its own Shangri-la Wine Company. Moët owns two-thirds of the venture and took a fifty-year lease on select vineyards scattered over four villages, including Adong, home to the winery. Leasing the land from farmers, rather than paying them for grapes by weight, allowed the French to grow grapes as they saw fit. On top of rent, the company offered its landlords the opportunity to get paid working the vineyard under supervision. The more land farmers leased to Moët, the more hours they could work for them. This is much like the land-lease arrangements from Shandong and Hebei that we talked about earlier in the book. Brendan's research shows that the French company offered villagers a better deal overall,[6] which makes sense when you consider the long-term investment required by Moët Hennessy's most expensive wine estate in the world.[7]

Everything was just perfect. Except the fact that it was in the middle of nowhere. Looking back at our little van's journey through the mountains from Shangri-la, we felt for the truck drivers in charge of getting winery supplies all the way up there, and the finished bottles back on their way to key markets in big Chinese cities and the world. The arduous paths to the vineyards, with blocks spread across four different villages, must make harvest interesting. No wonder the project is so expensive.

Lunchtime was approaching. We'd had a great time learning about the family and taking pictures of vineyard views, and we even walked by Moët's winery. Everyone stayed professional and followed the boss's orders (no visitors inside). Without our dream VIP invitation in hand, and with our driver waiting, Pierre still thought we were about to say good-bye. But that's when our hosts mentioned that we should stay for lunch. Some of the winery's technical staff, including an "American," they said, were on their way to have lunch in the dining room. In fact, they didn't just eat here every day; they lived in the guestrooms upstairs. The family home, one of several guesthouses in the village, served, it turns out, as a local staff dorm that happened to have two vacant rooms just for us.

* * *

Pierre learned to appreciate Cynthia's idea of fieldwork even more around the lunch table. With no official invitation from up high, he couldn't have dreamed we would be sharing a meal and good conversation with Gavin, one of the young vineyard managers, and his colleague, a graduate from Kunming University working on quality control. Mid-twenties, casually dressed for a hard day walking several miles up and down Moët's vineyards, Gavin is the kind of guy you could meet on a University of California campus. Armed with a master's degree in viticulture and enology from the University of Adelaide in Australia, he worked a vintage in California's Sonoma County before taking a marketing job to explore another side of the wine business. But being a technical person at heart, he looked for a way back into the more hands-on vineyard and winemaking world, and somehow landed here in Adong village.

In fact, Gavin is not American at all. He is Chinese, born, raised, and educated all the way through his undergraduate years studying biotechnology in Beijing. His fluent English and global experience were enough for locals to refer to him as "the American," particularly since he doesn't speak Tibetan. As an undergrad, he wasn't a great student, he admitted. Learning to play drums, doing karate, and skateboarding sounded a lot more fun than spending late nights buried in textbooks. And he liked drinking too, mostly beer, and sometimes wine. His beginner wines were of the cheap kind, from big Chinese brands that you can find everywhere. But that was enough to get him interested, and he eventually got into wine graduate school in Adelaide.

Part of what made his job hard was all the walking across Moët's vineyards spread over four villages. After life in Beijing, Sonoma, and Adelaide, it's not every young college graduate's dream to spend months in a tiny village lost in the mountains. But Gavin seemed fascinated by the place. He felt his education prepared him well to adapt, and the opportunity to help a major wine brand crack the code to unfamiliar, extreme terroir was exciting. With the villages located over one hour's drive from each other, he explained, the differences in climate can be surprisingly important. Even within a single village, variations in elevation across vineyard blocks can lead to significant change in average temperatures. "When you consider that all the factors can have impact to viticulture, you can get incredible diversity from this region, and the diversity can be reflected in your wine," he told us in an email a year later.

As a vineyard manager, he was one of the key intermediaries between Moët's winemakers and local farmers. If he didn't do his job well, growers could miss crucial instructions and grapes would fail to meet the bosses' high expectations. It often took some convincing, since after all, locals had been growing grapes for years with their own understanding of the land before Moët showed up. The language barrier, especially with older growers who were less comfortable in Mandarin, didn't make Gavin's job any easier. But as a young wine professional, he always looked for new challenges, working different jobs in diverse conditions, in wineries large and small, famous and unknown. His advice to young wine peers: "Don't be a snob; it will limit you."

We had to ask about the top-secret wine in progress of course. Gavin thought it was good, though it was neither his job nor in his character to be effusive about it. All we knew was that it would be a Bordeaux blend, dominated by Cabernet Sauvignon. Critics who tasted Moët's first Shangri-la wine trials seemed very impressed. Jancis Robinson described "mountain wines, with the dense colour and vivid, finely etched flavours that you find in the high-altitude wines of Argentina or even in the best Ribera del Duero wines."[8] Although she had given good marks and very enthusiastic pats on the back to several Chinese wines before, the new words and comparisons chosen here went well beyond. *Decanter* magazine's Jane Anson was impressed too: "The wine is rich and ripe without sacrificing freshness. The quality of the tannins is what impresses me the most, soft but dense."[9]

"Is there any way we could . . ." Cynthia didn't get to finish her question. "No," Gavin said with polite but assertive finality, clearly assuming we were hoping to sample a barrel tasting. That's not where Cynthia was going with this, but okay, got it. We were lucky enough to stumble upon Moët staff on lunch break, and we didn't want anybody to risk their job. Although the company planned to release the first vintage in the United States and Europe, based on everything written about the place so far, we got the message: it was going to be scarce, very expensive, and Pierre being financially prudent anyway, it would never touch our lips.

Gavin's afternoon involved more walking the vineyards, but first, he had to pick up a colleague. We didn't expect it would be in Adong village, on the little road outside the Moët winery gate, that Pierre would use his broken Spanish for the first time in years. What was an Argentinean from Mendoza doing here? It's not as far-fetched as it sounds. Back in the 1950s, Moët & Chandon's chairman, Jean de Vogüé, knew that Champagne would soon face growing competition from other wine regions figuring out their own versions of quality sparkling wine. Ignoring many Champenois who thought they were crazy, Moët's team searched the world for suitable terroirs. In 1959, Bodegas Chandon, the first of the Champagne giant's ventures abroad, was born.

Luciano, a graduate from the National University of Cuyo and an agronomist at Bodegas Chandon with sixteen years of experience, remembered that day in January when he and other "tecnicos" were invited to a special dinner with Jean-Guillaume Prats, the CEO of Moët Hennessy's Estates and Wines division. Luciano had never met Prats, nor did he have any clue about the purpose of the evening. Imagine his surprise (and that of his fellow diners) when the big boss invited him to fill the empty seat next to his to show him pictures on his phone. It all made sense the next day, when he was offered the opportunity to spend three months on a mission in a very, very different kind of place.

So here he was, living in one of the winery's luxury guest apartments for top staff, spending his days assessing irrigation ditches and analyzing soil samples across vineyards, often with Gavin as his guide. At each stop with a soil pit ready for him to jump in, he scanned the layers of dirt and made a few comments in Spanish for his mini voice recorder. Later, he would analyze more results on his computer. All this would eventually help map the terroir precisely. Moët doesn't leave anything to guesswork. It was an opportunity that the Mendozan couldn't pass. He made friends with Chinese colleagues, learned to post pictures on WeChat, and enjoyed the place the best he could. But as fascinating as life in a small Chinese village can be, without a single Spanish speaker around, by the end of the summer, he must have started to count down the days. At night, he played guitar and called home to his young daughter and pregnant wife. Only a few weeks to go, and he would be home in time to welcome their son to the world.

We let Luciano and the American go about the rest of their day and planned to meet for dinner at "la casa del doctor," where we had settled in our rooms for the night. Our trusty Wine Check suitcase wasn't empty yet, and that night seemed like the perfect time to lighten it. "We brought a Washington wine. If you'd like, we would love to open it with you." "Por supuesto gracias." Back in the dining room where, a few hours earlier, we'd been almost ready to leave Adong, our dinner table was a fun but exhausting mix of languages. Cynthia collected little paper cups from everyone and poured what was perhaps the first (or at least among the very few) Washington wine ever opened in Adong village. Before he'd even seen the label, Gavin sniffed the Syrah from a mile away. Luciano posed for a picture holding the bottle with the signature little airplane label of Yakima Valley's Airfield Estates.

As the street got darker, the party moved upstairs to the couches around the common room's coffee table. Soon after Luciano said goodnight and headed back to his Moët dungeon, a young Chinese woman who had just gotten home took his spot and accepted our offer for a little Syrah, her first taste of Washington wine. A graduate from Kunming University but originally from Deqin closer to Shangri-la, she had been working with Moët for a month. Later into the night, more young Chinese employees arrived, including one doing an internship as part of her European wine master's degree. By now, Pierre had long gotten over his bitter feelings about the failed website contact request. What we found was so much better. We didn't care about meeting the boss, getting the VIP tour, or tasting secret wine samples. A dinner encounter in Bu village had led us to the Moët staff dorm, and we learned about a very different world of wine and wine tourism on the way.

9

BUBBLY ON THE ROCKS

"**H**ow about tomorrow morning 8:40 a.m., I pick you up and taste our 2015 wine, and then we visit other wineries?" We agreed, excited to see Liao, Zhang Yanzhi's young colleague in Ningxia, and thought we knew what to expect. Would we take selfies with a Changyu castle mascot? Would we walk by decorated stone walls toward a lavish tasting room with an exhibit celebrating a winery's success? We did some of that, of course. But it turns out Liao had much more interesting plans. "I want you to see something different," he said. In the afternoon, after parking in front of a beat-up temporary gate, Liao asked an old man on guard duty with his dog if we could visit the place. The guard let us in but gave us a bemused look as if he thought, *Really? You want to see that? Okay . . .* Sure, there were a couple of finished stone walls, and even some large windows overlooking vineyards. Other than that, we walked around an abandoned construction site. Inside, walls and staircases were still incomplete with bare cement. It wasn't clear when any of this would be finished, if ever.

That day, we drove by other struggling wineries. Liao explained that some even made good wine. Sometimes, an ambitious owner stocked the cellar with state-of-the-art equipment but ran out of money. Other times, a wealthy investor poured capital into buildings and machines, hired a great winemaker, but lacked wine marketing skills. With the famous success stories of Ningxia wine, it's too easy to forget a tough reality: wine, even good wine, doesn't sell itself. What if all this Chinese wine and wine tourism was a big mirage? Would our dreams of Ningxia wine vacations to come be shattered and replaced by visits to wine ghost towns instead?

The stalled construction sites forced us to really consider the failed projects we knew existed but had never actually seen. Still, Liao shared our optimism about many budding Ningxia wineries. After all, several local wineries are good marketers of their wines. Liao listed a few names. One of them brought back fond memories because it was part of our first Ningxia itinerary in 2013. Having landed in Yinchuan without a single local contact, we sat at our little Jinjiang Inn with a list of phone numbers. Our assistant Josephine made calls, often reaching no answer. But with some persistence, it took only a few hours to fill our week with appointments.

* * *

Wu Hongfu was smiling when he pulled up with his shiny black car in front of our Jinjiang Inn in Yinchuan. It was our first visit to Ningxia, and it would take three years for us to figure out we could find hotels closer to wine country. But the middle-aged winemaker kindly gave us the hour-long ride to his winery, Leirenshou. After many rides in beaten-up local taxis, we enjoyed the smooth and soothing feel of a nice car. Born and raised in southern China, after high school Mr. Wu applied to universities in the North so he could finally see snow. He was accepted into the second-ever graduating class at Li Hua's College of Enology in Yangling and, a few years later, came to work for Leirenshou. The winery, founded in 2002 and owned by a local, may not get as much attention in Western media as Grace Vineyard or Silver Heights, but it has built a strong brand locally and earned its share of international medals. So, as usual, we were taken aback when he took us to the lab and invited us to comment on several vintages with different types of oak aging, before improvising a blend to take to lunch.

From the start, Leirenshou benefited from local authorities' efforts to promote wine tourism. With bottle-shaped road signs pointing the way on nicely paved roads in the middle of the wine town in development, you couldn't miss the winery if you passed it. Not that it tried to be a grandiose French or Italian castle. The building was relatively simple, but the bright burgundy color and prominent "Leirenshou" letters at the top stood out in the middle of quiet rural roads and vineyards. Conveniently located a short ride from other wineries (each with their own bottle-shaped sign), the winery could easily offer programs for visitors. At one harvest festival, guests put on matching Leirenshou jackets, picked grapes, and crushed them by hand, before gathering on the patio for a roast lamb lunch. Happy people going home with fond memories, wine, and pictures to share with friends could become free brand ambassadors, a great asset in a market where people care about recommendations from people they know and trust.

One hundred percent geared to Chinese consumers, Leirenshou's marketing used references to Ningxia's history and culture. Many labels featured the local mountain, a classic way to convey a terroir message in many wine regions of the world. But the ones that really caught our attention were those depicting reproductions of several rock engravings from the Helan Mountain caves tourist site. In fact, at the top of the building, an image of the famous *Sun God* rock carving stood for the letter *O* in *Leirenshou*. We found the labels memorable because they told a story about the place.

Another part of the marketing strategy was to submit wines at international competitions. There was much to celebrate when the 2009 Cabernet Sauvignon won a silver medal at the 2012 Decanter World Wine Awards, with a tasting note like this: "Attractive black berry fruit nose with toasted new French oak sweetness. Opulent on the palate with smoky tannins and refreshing acidity. Intense, rich." Other awards followed, including one at the 2015 Concours Mondial de Bruxelles.

Outside of the ubiquitous large-scale producers, many local wines were hard to find. So we were pleasantly surprised to run into Leirenshou wines at Yinchuan supermarkets, convenience stores, and even some local barbecue restaurants where the wine list was otherwise limited. Before lunch, Mr. Wu wanted to show us the people who made it happen. Relaxing at a park a short drive from the winery, young sales reps were barbecuing lamb with their families and pouring wine straight from jugs. Within minutes of our arrival, parents were eager to have their children pose for pictures and share toasts to the group's success. Many of these reps worked directly with supermarkets to make sure the brand was visible to mass-market consumers.

With the aura of recognition among the international wine intelligentsia, some suggested they could raise prices. But they preferred not to, keeping a range of wines decidedly in the mass-market category, starting as low as sixty-eight yuan (about ten dollars). Leirenshou had enough volume to offer a wide range of prices for different market segments, another key strength when award-winning local wines could be very expensive. All this was possible thanks not only to grapes grown on 2,000 mu (about 330 acres) of vineyards they owned but also to twice as much fruit bought from eighty individual household farms on long-term contracts, including bonuses for higher quality. It all looked like a well-oiled machine. At least we could be sure Leirenshou was successful enough to be around the next time we come. But how many wineries could combine talent in both making good wine and selling it? The construction sites and many rumors about unsold inventories in the region gave us pause.

*　*　*

We felt a little out of place eating Spanish food in the Sanlitun neighborhood of Beijing in 2014. Our dinner at Migas, a Spanish restaurant with a fun menu and original house-made desserts, was lovely. But we weren't here to satisfy a paella craving. Migas carried Chateau Nine Peaks, a winery from Shandong we hadn't been able to visit, and we hoped to buy some. Of course, most customers here chose Spanish wine, but the general manager, Juan, thought a restaurant in China should have a Chinese wine. And it helped that the distributor, East Meets West Fine Wines, eager to promote one of only two Chinese brands in its portfolio, offered the first six bottles for free. At tables around us, young to middle-aged Chinese diners, from couples on romantic dates to girls' night out, all sipped European wines, which made sense. At the time, many observers noted that China's wine market had been shifting, from one based on a search for status to price-conscious drinkers who liked the taste. We wondered what it would take for Chinese wine to be popular at this kind of venue. But sitting down for a chat with Juan and his young restaurant's wine expert, Fangfang, we ended up learning about something completely different, something that had more important implications for Chinese wineries' sales.

Supermarkets were filled with large-scale mass-market brands, but were our favorite Chinese wines, the ones everybody was talking about, generally accessible to savvy Chinese shoppers? Juan, who had lived in China only a year, spoke with the unmistakable victory of a foreigner who had found the secret to share with other foreigners. "Taobao!" he said, as if he couldn't verbalize as many exclamation points as he wanted.

"Anything you want to buy, go to Taobao. You'll need a Chinese person, but you can get anything. Imagine *anything* you might want to buy. Those lights. That chalkboard. These glasses. All from Taobao," he said, pointing to almost every piece of restaurant equipment in sight. Fangfang added, "You can probably get Chinese wine." Plus, the shipping is almost always free.

The free shipping thing was something we'd never wrapped our heads around, and we made a point to ask a Chinese marketing executive about it later. "Chinese people don't like to pay for shipping," he told us. Well, neither do we, but tell Jeff Bezos that and you end up with a monthly subscription to Amazon Prime. If we lived in China, we could buy several of our favorite Chinese wines online from just about anywhere in the country, with little to no shipping cost. Given the growing importance of e-commerce for imported wine,[1] it could be crucial for Chinese wineries too, especially those award-winning ones that you don't easily run into while shopping in brick-and-mortar stores.

Counterfeit goods were a problem though, Juan warned. But if you ordered something you didn't like, you could usually return it for any reason. We could still hear the exclamation points in the Spaniard's voice. The question of product authenticity was serious, and imports weren't the only victims. Renowned Ningxia winemakers Zhang Jing and Emma Gao both told us their brands and labels had been copied. But there was more than one kind of online store, and some tried to provide guarantees. Taobao was only one side of e-commerce giant Alibaba. They also had Tmall, where brands could set up their own shop. Even the NBA and the NFL opened one. On Tmall, wineries like Grace Vineyard or Leirenshou could not only sell wine directly but also tell their stories. On Leirenshou's Tmall store, you could not only find all the wines but also learn about the winery and the story behind the rock-carving labels, watch pictures and videos, and read advice on how to make the most out of the wine life: a glass for lunch for happiness, more at 3:00 p.m. for afternoon tea, some more with dinner, and finally, a 9:00 p.m. sip to relax before bed. An employee even seemed to have been assigned to respond to any poor customer ratings in a positive way.

Tmall vetted applicants, verified brand ownership, and more generally, invested in fraud detection. For Chinese wineries, selling direct helped build trust and signal authenticity, but it came at a hefty price. Not all producers could afford the thousands of dollars for a one-time security deposit, plus annual service fees and commission.

There were a few people we had in mind who surely didn't have that kind of money. One of them was a young guy named Jianjun, whom we'd first met on a 2015 Ningxia visit at Silver Heights, where he worked. A year later, we caught up with him at a delightful Xinjiang cuisine restaurant in Yinchuan, where older men performed traditional music and dances, swaying between tables, while young women in Uighur dresses served food. We drank a bottle of his wine and were blown away by his story. Originally from Henan Province, Jianjun worked in IT after his university degree in sociology but quickly learned that wasn't his thing. A bit of a hipster, with long hair, an art museum T-shirt, and a love for poetry and literature, it was hard to imagine him doing anything other than winemaking or art. Back in his IT days, he read about wine tasting and winemaking and got hooked. He particularly enjoyed the writing of a famous Ningxia winemaker who'd studied in Burgundy, France. That's how he learned about wineries in Ningxia and soon decided to write Emma Gao of Silver Heights to ask for a job. It worked.

He packed up what little he had and traveled to Yinchuan. When he called to confirm his first day, no one answered. His stomach turned. What if he came all this way for nothing? He took a deep breath and showed up unannounced at the little urban winery to introduce himself. For four years, Jianjun, who had never studied wine formally or made a drop of wine, learned everything he could from Emma Gao and her husband Thierry Courtade at Silver Heights. He even picked a French name: Gustave, after French writer Gustave Flaubert.

After he developed back problems, he had to slow down and eventually quit the job. But that opened the path to his next step: making his own wine. He bought grapes from farmers and, with a little help from friends and contacts, made two thousand bottles. Unable to afford new oak, he used oak staves and old barrels for his first vintage. And true to his other passion, he designed the label to tell a story of Ningxia through one of his favorite poets. There was no doubt Jianjun was talented and enterprising, but as a single thirty-one-year-old with no family in Ningxia, no winery, and not even an office, how could he possibly sell his wine and make a living?

That wasn't the first time we asked ourselves this question. At least Ningxia had a booming wine sector and lots of infrastructure. And Jian-

Jianjun describing his wines.

jun lived in the region's capital, Yinchuan. But do you remember Bu village, in Tibetan Yunnan? It's still Cynthia's favorite place in China, and the first where we really encountered the "how can they possibly sell wine" question. Farmer and winemaker Zhuge lived there, five hours away from any airport, in this beautiful but poor village nested in high mountains. When we visited, she had long sold the last of her flagship product, a local ice wine. Selling didn't seem to be a problem for her at all. So, the big question was, how on earth did she get wine to her customers? Even with good grapes, business acumen, and adventure travelers stopping by, there was just no way we could imagine. She answered in one word.

"Weidian." You see, in Chinese, WeChat, the ubiquitous social media platform with almost a billion users, is known as *Weixin*. And *dian* means shop. With a cell phone and a social network that she maintained on WeChat, she could keep up with contacts, take orders, receive payments, and ship her wine anywhere. So, when an American visitor who had visited Bu village was back in Beijing, he had no problem ordering

Zhuge's Yunnan ice wine. On WeChat, every year, Zhuge posted beautiful pictures of her vineyards, as well as updates on harvest and winemaking, and then let everyone know wine was ready for sale. In fact, many farmers around the country used WeChat to sell their produce this way.

Back in Ningxia, Jianjun did the same thing, although he took it one step further. WeChat allowed people not only to receive payments (friends could send each other money too) but also to set up an actual online shop. On his, Jianjun shared his story, writing (one of his artsy hobbies), pictures, and wines. Jianjun's production was small enough, and he had enough of a name, that he could sell all his wines this way.

We loved that even small and medium producers could succeed, each in their own way, and it gave us hope for the many more who made good wine. Unsurprisingly, Liao's list of Ningxia successes wasn't limited to Chinese brands. We also found a name familiar to many Champagne and sparkling wine lovers around the world, one with an excellent track record in the sales game.

* * *

In two days, our research assistant Dora, a twenty-something graduate student from Fuzhou, must have tasted more wine than she'd ever had in her life to date. One Ningxia winery visit after the next, she had patiently played along with the tastings, mostly reds and some whites. She always had plenty left to pour out in the dump bucket. In part, of course, she wanted to keep her interpreter's mind sharp and clear. She was genuinely curious and even asked her own questions about the wines from time to time. But we knew they weren't her first choice of drink.

This time was different. Somewhere in the middle of conversation with our host, we noticed Dora's glass was empty. She smiled, looking happy but embarrassed: "I like their sparkling wine very much!" That this visit would be the one when Dora drank faster than we did was perhaps no coincidence. Oh, Dora, they knew you were coming. Well, not you specifically, but young, educated people who enjoy a good time and things that taste good. Moët Hennessy Louis Vuitton did not create their Ningxia line of bubblies without a good dose of market research.

Dora remembered the time she had Moët & Chandon Champagne with a friend and liked it a lot. But at a price range from three to five hundred yuan a bottle, she and her friends, who were just getting started professionally, could hardly order it for karaoke night. Other Champagne brands that LVMH owns, such as Krug or Veuve Cliquot, were no cheaper. And don't even think about Moët's flagship vintage Champagne, Dom Pérignon, which would set you back a thousand yuan or more.

The good news for Dora and her friends was that they made the bubbly she loved in Ningxia just as it could be in Champagne, but it cost half the price or less. First, base still wines were made from Pinot Noir and Chardonnay grapes (two of the varieties allowed in Champagne), and the team concocted a blend. Then, they added a little yeast and sugar. The result was bottled and left to ferment a second time, in the bottle, which trapped carbon dioxide and made the bubbles happen. Finally, after a little aging to develop flavor, the dead yeast sediment was removed and the sweetness level was adjusted to the desired house style. This is called the traditional method, and that's what they do in Champagne. Don't call this Ningxia bubbly "Champagne" though, or you will hear from the region's lawyers. "Champagne" can only come from the Champagne region of France. This one is sparkling wine, brought to you by Domaine Chandon in Ningxia.

In the entrance, an ornamental tribute to the brand's history reminded visitors that it was far from the first time Moët made sparkling wine abroad. Topped by the signature Chandon logo, a bottle sat surrounded by six small golden circles, each showing the name of a place and a year: Argentina 1959, Brazil 1973, California 1973, Australia 1986, India 2013, and China 2013. The China project was the latest offspring in the global family. From the top of the winery, the Hollywood-like big white letters of CHANDON looked almost photoshopped, floating on top of the vineyard, and stamping the multinational brand on the views of Helan Mountain. We were right off the G110, by the way, close to Chateau Yunmo, the winery where we once arrived two hours late for dinner with the boss after our taxi took a wrong turn.

A small tractor brought in small bins of Pinot Noir grapes as we walked outside in the back. Busy employees who, like us, wore obligatory orange and yellow reflective jackets, cleaned the floor in preparation for the crush to come, and women in white coats worked in the immaculate lab. Meanwhile, two French photographers (part of the PR machine, we assumed) took pictures from the top of stainless-steel fermentation tanks. Having done this a few times around the globe, LVMH knew what they were doing, from growing grapes to selling wine. Still, the hardest

Chandon Ningxia.

part, our host Su Long explained, was maintaining a healthy relationship with the local government.

To get the required permits and a lease for more than sixty-six hectares where they planted Pinot Noir and Chardonnay, Moët Hennessy went into a joint venture with the state-owned Ningxia Nongken corporation, a key gatekeeper to access land. The Ningxia government was, as we've mentioned before, very supportive of wine, seeing it as a tool for economic development and tax revenue. But a new winery, even one by LVMH, didn't turn land into cash as quickly as coal or real estate. So, at every board meeting, the team had to make the case that this was all worth it and explain why success in wine required a long-term perspective.

Every bit of this had been researched to death. A thorough market study helped find the right style, sweetness level, targets for production volume, and pricing, for the white and rosé versions of the Brut. Investments in the winery balanced high-quality expectations and eco-friendliness with a controlled budget that made competitive prices possible.

About half the grapes were bought in from a government-run farm, which not only helped reach the desired volume but also provided access to quality grapes from vines older than those of the estate.

"We are innovating for consumers who don't like the traditional taste of Chandon," said the global president of Chandon, Davide Marcovitch, in an interview with Bloomberg.[2] And innovative they were. Since our visit, the company launched a new line called Chandon Me, a play on the Chinese term for honey, *mi*, which sounds like "me." Customers didn't even need an ice bucket to enjoy the fruity, slightly sweet Chandon Me. The back label listed no-fuss serving temperatures: (1) room temperature; (2) chilled; and (3) on the rocks. It all worked. In fact, if that's your thing, please go ahead and make cocktails with it. While this kind of language may not evoke high quality for wine snobs, Chandon Me earned a silver medal at the 2017 Decanter World Wine Awards.

Of course, LVMH had an additional incentive to push their Ningxia wines. Expanding the market for sparkling wine in China could boost their sales of Champagne, the more expensive kind that can only be made in Champagne, France.

Can you believe that on September 5, 2011, Moët celebrated, with much glamour, its 168th year in China? They'd been there since 1843, exactly one hundred years after the company was founded. For the occasion, Moët hosted the "dîner du siècle," as the press release put it, and launched a cork-shaped hot-air balloon on a journey through Beijing, the Great Wall, and Shanghai. Moët's brand ambassador, Scarlett Johansson, flew in for the Shanghai party, along with other celebrities, and the rooftop of the Peninsula Hotel was "specially crafted with fifteen thousand Champagne glasses."[3]

Given Champagne's global marketing success as the top wine representative of luxury and glamour, you'd think it'd be very popular in wealthy China. Except not really. The *dîner du siècle* may keep Champagne flowing for a night, but overall, sparkling wine lagged far behind still wine growth in China, both in volume and value. Observers offered various reasons for this, including the lack of a place for sparkling wine in a banquet setting, the lack of Champagne glasses in people's homes, and the taste,[4] although all of these could be said about still wine as well. In any case, interest in sparkling wine was growing, and Chandon Ningxia planned to both build on and fuel the trend.

You see, LVMH did whatever it took to get Dora and her friends to drink more bubbly: hot-air balloons, celebrity rooftop extravaganzas, sponsorships of Honda Formula One car racing, and yes, even Ningxia sparkling wine on the rocks. The fact that a company with such a strong history of successful marketing around the world put serious effort into selling Ningxia wine gave us further hope that the local wine economy wasn't just a mirage. And they weren't even the first French multinational to get into the Ningxia wine game.

* * *

"Woaaaaahhh!" Novak Djokovic raised both fists in the air, screaming his lungs out with pride, and threw a ball to the other side of the court. The tennis champion's win of the day was no small feat. After many failed attempts, he had finally done it, with the help of a patient coach. In a moment caught on camera, and now seen by more than one hundred thousand viewers on YouTube, he had managed to say, in perfect standard Mandarin tones: *He wo yiqi zhichi Jiekasi.* In English: Together with me, support Jacobs Creek.

You may have heard of Jacobs Creek, the immensely popular mega wine brand from Australia. It was a big hit in China too. The 2014 China Food and Drink Fair index ranked it fourth among imported wine brands, only topped by French legendary Lafite as number one, Bordeaux's giant wine group Castel, and another big Australian success story, Penfolds. According to the index, Jacobs Creek even beat Moët & Chandon Champagne, Chateau Petrus, and Opus One, among other wine elites.[5] This success didn't happen by chance. Pernod Ricard, the French multinational drinks conglomerate that has owned Jacobs Creek since 1989, knew how to sell wines and spirits. You would surely recognize a few of their brands, such as Jameson Irish Whiskey, Chivas Regal, or Absolut Vodka.

For the Chinese market, there was no way around making poor Novak Djokovic work on his Chinese tones to use Jacobs Creek's Chinese name. Chinese names for foreign brands were very important, and we found out the hard way. One morning in Beijing, we went on what was supposed to be a quick shopping trip to Carrefour, the French supermarket chain. With perfectly prepared Chinese sentences, we directed the taxi driver to the famous brand: "We are going to Carrefour." We don't remember where we landed, but Carrefour was nowhere to be seen. That easy errand quickly turned into an aimless three-hour walk, including a failed stop at the Novotel, where even English-speaking Chinese staff couldn't possibly figure out what we were looking for. We eventually stumbled upon Carrefour, and now we know. We'd prepared the "We are going to" part, but Carrefour? That meant nothing to our driver. You must ask for *Jialefu* or show your driver the Chinese characters.

It's a great name, by the way. *Jia* means family; *le*, happy; and *fu*, good fortune, a nice combination. For famous brands trying to make it in China, one of many challenges involves finding a great Chinese name. Coca-Cola hadn't come up with one yet when the soft drink was first sold in China in 1927, so local shopkeepers took on the task, trying to assemble characters that sounded like Coca-Cola to them. Somehow, this led Coke to be known on some streets as something that loosely translated as "bite the wax tadpole," or even "female horse fastened with wax," not exactly great marketing.[6] Next time you order a Coke in China, you'll use their much better trademark, *kekou kele*, which evokes tasty and happy. Many observers speculate that Chateau Lafite owes part of its Chinese success to its local name, *Lafei*, which sounds good and rolls off the tongue.

Linguist entrepreneur John Pasden joked back in 2006, after seeing Jacobs Creek ads playing in the Shanghai subway, that from an English speaker's perspective, *Jiekasi* sounded more like, well, jackass than Jacobs Creek.[7] But that would only be a problem if the intended Chinese audience was really into American slang. The first character means "outstanding," and combined with the other two, sure, it sounds about right, and it's easy for consumers to pronounce. It seems to have worked just fine for the Australian wine brand so far.

And they didn't just get Novak to say *Jiekasi*. That was just part of the outtakes of "Made By," a series of poignant Jacobs Creek ads with the "Djoker" telling his life story, from his childhood when he made a pretend Wimbledon trophy to the time he first won it for real. There was a Chinese version, of course, with a local narrator and subtitles for Novak's lines. But what was it about Novak? Why not choose Roger Federer or Rafael Nadal? We think there were a few reasons. On top of six Australian Open titles, he'd won the China Open six times. While other top players picked up *nihao* (hello) and *xiexie* (thank you), Novak, who can give competent TV interviews in German, Italian, French, Spanish, and his native Serbian, worked on a few more Chinese sentences. The crowd went crazy when he said "nihao" in one on-court interview after a win, so imagine how much louder they got when he followed with "wo ai nimen" (I love you all) and "wo ai zhongguo" (I love China). Instead of merely signing his autograph on the courtside camera, he regaled viewers with his favorite Chinese characters.[8] He held a live Q&A with Chinese fans on the local messaging app QQ and was active on Weibo, the Chinese social media platform. And he based his diet, in part, on traditional Chinese medicine. Novak was a fantastic choice if you were serious about selling Australian wine in China, something that was getting increasingly important thanks to the free-trade agreement between Australia and China, ChAFTA.

But what did all this have to do with Chinese wine? The good news for our future Ningxia wine vacation prospects was that the Pernod Ricard PR machine also decided to make and sell local wine. We visited the winery in 2013, and it's time to take you back there with us.

* * *

It must have been quite a scene when a thousand visitors, glass in hand, elbowed their way to the board to place tiny yellow sticky notes in the column that best described their impressions of the 2011 Helan Mountain Special Reserve Chardonnay. A week later, the board was still there for us to see, and the verdict was clear: many dots in the "good" column, but so many more under "excellent" that you could barely see the background anymore. Good thing they loved it, because that was part of the pitch for this gigantic sales crew in charge of placing Pernod Ricard products around China, including Martell Cognac and Jacobs Creek.

With vineyards first planted in 1996 and the facility built a year later, Ningxia's Helan Mountain winery has been around since well before the French multinational came along. Pernod Ricard joined as a partner in 2007 and put the group's chief winemaker, Philip Laffer, in charge. The year 2007 had seen the winery's biggest grape harvest, fourteen tons, but winemaker Mr. Liu told us the new approach would soon bring yields down and quality up. Many of the grapes came from the winery's own vineyards, though they also bought a little from farmers under contract who received detailed guidance from vineyard managers. To keep export options open, only pesticides approved in the United States were used. We didn't think exports outside China were the main motivation behind Helan Mountain winery, but we hoped they'd take that extra step someday.

In 2012, Pernod Ricard took advantage of friendlier rules for foreign investors, to do what earlier joint ventures often couldn't: they bought their partner's shares and became the sole owner. The renamed winery, Pernod Ricard Helan Mountain, now led by another Aussie winemaker, Craig Grafton, was doing well. It sold thirty-one thousand cases in China in 2016 and earned medals at international wine competitions. We couldn't disagree with the thousand sales staff as we tried the latest batch of finished Chardonnay. Master of wine Jeannie Cho Lee called the 2011 a "serious Chardonnay with lovely mixed nuts and ripe peach and melon flavors."[9] And the Pinot Noir, our first in China, was lovely too.

Consumers could order Helan Mountain wines on the winery's online Tmall store (the same platform Leirenshou used). "Built in 1997, a product of the Pernod Ricard group," the top banner says in Chinese. Next, e-visitors could scroll down to explore options. The entry-level 2013 Cabernet Sauvignon only cost seventy-eight yuan, about twelve dollars, a very competitive price for quality Chinese wine. Those looking for a nice gift could buy the two-pack for 188 yuan, which came in a beautiful red box wrapped in a Helan Mountain gift bag, with a corkscrew and a bottle stopper. And splurge options were available too: 158 yuan for one bottle of their premium Cab, or the dinner party set of six bottles of premium Chardonnay for 752 yuan.

Once shoppers made their choice, the next step was to move down the page to learn more and check the customer reviews. They didn't have to scroll very far to get a message in big font: Helan Mountain wine was part of the Pernod Ricard family of brands, including Martell Cognac, Chivas Whiskey, Jacobs Creek, and more. Customers who came for the Chinese wine were inundated with international brand logos. So maybe soon they would also visit the general Pernod Ricard Tmall store and realize that Jacobs Creek was affordable. And the video of a young couple having the Merlot while making dumplings at home together was pretty darn cute.

The online store for Chandon Me had the same thing. Customers landed at Moët Hennessy's retail page, on another platform called JD.com, where they were inundated with possibilities. Veuve Cliquot Champagne? Hennessy Cognac? The group's famous brands were all a click away.

At first, we wondered if Helan Mountain winery, for all its merits, was really a tool to promote imported brands. But they seemed serious about it. The website of the group's wine division, Pernod Ricard Winemakers, placed Helan Mountain prominently on their list of "Global Icons," along with Jacobs Creek, New Zealand's Brancott Estate, or Spain's Campo Viejo, all common offerings at major US supermarkets.

Seeing successful Chinese wines made by locals, global conglomerates, and even individual farmers with tiny inventories on WeChat, we were hopeful for the future. Our Ningxia wine vacations may come true after all, even if a few enterprises fail along the way. Now if only Pernod Ricard could place some Helan Mountain wines in a few supermarkets in the United States. In the meantime, our Chinese wine supply was dependent on the trusty wine suitcase we filled before every return flight home.

10

FILLING OUR WINE SUITCASE

With only a couple of days left at the end of our first Chinese wine expedition, we were ready to buy our favorite wines to take home. We planned to serve them at tastings and tell other travelers where to find them in Beijing. We had an address, but two hours after landing in the neighborhood, well past lunchtime, we weren't quite there. It would have been nice to have more than one store to choose from. With all the attention that the best boutique Chinese wines had been getting for several years, we figured they'd be easy to find in their home country. Well, to be fair, they just weren't easy to find *for us*.

Giant producers, such as Changyu and Great Wall, spent years building their brands through TV and radio advertising, and established a stronghold on the main distribution channels. No matter what convenience store or supermarket we went to, we'd see the same big names. Other than megabrands, you couldn't just run into the wines we've mentioned in this book. Without a Chinese bank account (only available to residents), online shopping was not an option. To fill our trusty Wine Check suitcase, we had to get lost in subways, engage in confusing exchanges with taxi drivers, and take unnecessarily long walks.

"One Frappuccino Blended Beverage," the barista announced, using the obligatory Starbucks name that is remarkably difficult to pronounce. Close to giving up, we needed Starbucks on that hot Beijing afternoon, not so much for the coffee but for the Wi-Fi. Dying to find Everwines, the only shop we knew that carried Grace Vineyard and Silver Heights, we got on our tablets and tried to map the place one more time. Across from the Bentley car dealership, one website said. "Wait, we are right next to the dealership!" But we had walked across the block for a while, asking in other stores, and failed to find it for two hours (hint: the Chinese name of Everwines might have helped). We wouldn't have the luxury of GPS navigation for another year, when our research assistant finally used her mom's online shopping account to help us transition from our dinosaur-age flip phones. So, we used the Wi-Fi, downed our coffee, walked across the street, and there it was, just one level below the street, where we forgot to look.

Everwines was the retail arm of Torres China, with locations in several big cities across the country. The cozy Beijing location was both a wine shop and a bar, but the most important business happened in the office in the back: import and distribution. If you like Spanish wine, you may have heard about Torres, the global wine giant from Spain. Torres China imported Spanish wine of course, but also wines from thirteen other countries. They were even the exclusive importer for our Washington State wine giant, Chateau Ste Michelle. So how did our favorite Chinese wines end up in the shop? Torres's interest in Chinese wine went back to their entry into China, in 1997, when they established a winery joint venture in Hebei. One of their goals was to use the bottling line for their entry-level Spanish brand, Sangre de Toro, and importing wine into the country became the focus a few years later as China lowered import duties. But the local wine interest didn't go away. Torres had been an important supporter of Grace for many years, distributing a wide range of their wines at Everwines, and even collaborating on one, the Symphony, an off-dry Muscat meant to be an introduction for new wine drinkers. [1]

The Silver Heights connection was from the time winemaker Emma Gao started her wine business immersion by working as Torres's wine trainer in Shanghai. It was about when the family's first vintage was sitting in barrels. The company's general manager, Alberto Fernandez, loved it, and the rest is history. They helped come up with the winery's name and successfully placed the wines on the lists of nice hotels and restaurants. [2] Of course, since Torres's main business was imported wines, we wondered why they chose to carry Chinese wine at all. Who was interested? Sarah, a member of the Beijing Torres team, had a simple answer for us: mostly foreigners. That was only one part of the story of course, but one that we heard elsewhere too.

Thanks to Everwines, we had some of the best wines from China to share back home. Since that first adventure finding the shop, we have recommended it to anyone who asked us how they could find good Chinese wine during their upcoming trip to Beijing. We should give you an update though. While you would still find Silver Heights wines at Everwines, Grace moved on to become the only Chinese wine in the portfolio of another important distributor, ASC. We're not sure what it means for their availability, although ASC's strong presence means likely good news. Meanwhile, we needed more wine from more producers. And we had a new go-to Beijing wine shop for that.

* * *

We were at Pudao, a great Beijing wine shop, for serious research, of course. But excuse us if we can never resist the call of the enomatic machine. You buy a card, charge credit on it, and drain it from tap to tap getting tasting pours of wines of the world. What's not to like? Pudao offered sixteen wines on their enomatic machine and rotated them every couple of weeks to keep things interesting. This was the kind of thing that could keep us hanging out in the comfy seats longer than we planned. We took notes while we watched serious wine shopping in action. A couple walked in, and the wife went to sit down and play with her phone while hubby browsed around the whole store, looked at the Ridge display (a top California brand), and got some recommendations from the store attendant. A few minutes in, the wife joined the treasure hunt. Discussion and smiles ensued. She pointed to a bottle and said, "What about this one?" It was Eroica Riesling from Washington, a wine we love and were pleasantly surprised to see there.

The browsing continued, the store attendant took notes, and the wine enthusiast couple left with a world tour in three cases and two complimentary bottles of Perrier. After they left, Pierre had to ask the store attendant, were they planning a big event? Nope, this was to drink themselves. They're regulars. "Chinese people drink a lot. It's a good market," she explained. Pudao was a great atmosphere for an interview and a tasting, but we were there because they carried good Chinese wines. And like Everwines, they sold them mostly to foreigners. We could relate. After all, we found them because we were looking for one of our favorite Ningxia wines from Kanaan, headed by charismatic Crazy Fang. We took you there earlier in this book. Although Kanaan wines were our goal of the day, we didn't mind staying for enomatic tasting pours of premium red Burgundies. Could serious Chinese Burgundy enthusiasts have the mirror experience—come for the imports but learn to love their country's wines, with Kanaan as an introduction?

Kanaan had been getting attention for a while, including from Jancis Robinson, and yet, until recently, you couldn't find it without going to the winery. Blogger Jim Boyce, a Kanaan fan, took on the task of selling a few bottles himself, with the help of his friendly neighborhood wine shop, La Cava de Laoma. He announced the deal on his blog and social media accounts: come to La Cava to buy impossible-to-find Kanaan wines at the bargain price of one hundred yuan.[3] We loved this kind of enthusiasm, but it was not going to be a sustainable business proposition for even the best Chinese wineries.

Kanaan wines landed at Pudao thanks to a deal with Summergate, a major importer and distributor of drinks (including Perrier), owned by the Australian Woolworths Liquor Group. Pudao was their retail arm, but they knew where else to market Kanaan wines. Luxury restaurant and hotel groups like Shangri-la and Kempinski faced a niche demand from foreign tourists or business travelers curious to try Chinese wine. And if they didn't already have a name in mind, Summergate knew what to recommend. Now, of course, unless curious travelers were in a large group willing to share, they would probably not buy a whole expensive bottle just for a taste. To make sure Kanaan sold well, Summergate emphasized sales by the glass, offering good-enough deals so that restaurants could break even on each bottle after just a couple of glasses poured.

It was interesting that foreigners' curiosity would be the main motive for top distributors like Torres and Summergate to take on Chinese wines. But at least that made them available somewhere. And once they were on menus, and at Pudao, Chinese consumers hopefully ran into them too. In fact, that day, we realized Pudao had more than we thought. We found Ningxia's Helan Qingxue, Silver Heights, and even Xinjiang's Tiansai wine, which we'd never tried. Here they were, ready to fill half of our wine suitcase in one trip. Unfortunately, Pudao closed its Beijing outlet in June 2019. Sigh. But our search for more wines took us to the kind of place that more Chinese consumers were likely to visit than a small wine shop: a supermarket.

* * *

We went to Metro, a German retail chain with many outlets in China, to find not only Chandon's Ningxia sparkling wine but also a Xinjiang brand called 1421 Wines. We'd learned about them a year earlier in the coffee lounge of a swanky hotel lobby, across from the company's Beijing office, where Randy Svendsen and Ashley Gao met us. The main owner of 1421 Wines, Andrónico Luksic, happened to be the vice chairman of Banco de Chile and led the expansion of his family conglomerate into China.[4] Coming second was Johnny Chan, a Hong Kong businessman and TV food personality. Conveniently, since many clients were hotels and restaurants, Mr. Chan occasionally promoted them in his shows and made sure the camera didn't miss shots of 1421 bottles. Together, they were the VIP face of the brand.

Randy joined them after a different career. Since 1999, he had worked in China's manufacturing sector but got laid off after his last contract expired. With the global financial crisis, nobody was hiring in manufacturing in 2009. When the opportunity came along, he used his life savings to buy some of Chan's 1421 shares and became part owner. His job was to handle sales from the Beijing office. He was very happy with the work of his colleague Ashley, a wine expert he hired away from her previous job at a Chinese winery. Armed with cool PowerPoint presentations and educational wine aroma kits, she offered staff training for the winery's clients.

1421 Wines weren't meant to compete with boutique producers like Grace or Silver Heights, Randy said, adding that they were all fighting for the same cause. The point was to get consumers to consider smaller brands in the first place. Thanks to a supply chain that permitted large volumes, 1421 could sell entry-level wines for under one hundred yuan, making them competitive not only with the big local players but also with many mid-priced imports. For this to be possible, the wine went through quite a journey. It all started in the vineyards of northern Xinjiang, just north of the Tian Shan mountains. Unlike in the region's south, it rained enough, and winter brought a fresh source of snowmelt irrigation water. But there was no "1421 winery," per se, in Xinjiang. The company had a deal with a very large local producer who had access to a lot of grapes. A portion of the vineyards were contracted to make 1421 wines on site, vinified in huge tanks. Then, the wine was packed in large bladders, where it stayed protected from oxygen, and shipped on trucks to a winery facility all the way to Shandong Province on the east coast. There, 1421 winemaking crew handled final processing tasks like fining and aging in barrels. The winery kept a large quantity of wine in the large bladders for stability and only handled and bottled when they knew it could be sold.

A key feature of the 1421 brand was traceability, tapping into Chinese consumers' growing concerns about product origin and food safety. It worked through Metro's own traceability system, Star Farm, a consulting firm for agriculture that the Metro group founded in 2007. Consumers could scan the QR code on the bottle or go to Metro's website and type the label's traceability number under the bar code.[5] This led to a page of the Star Farm website dedicated to 1421, where they found information about the winery and its suppliers and vineyards, screenshots of official regulatory audits, and details on mode of transport (trucks, in this case) and the shipping route their wine had traveled.

We checked in with Randy recently to get the latest news. The 1421 Wines story continues, although with a few important changes. The Xinjiang wines are now bottled on site before shipping, to simplify logistics. And the brand has expanded to include imported wines from Chile, Australia, Italy, Spain, and France.

Over time, we got more creative in our search for wine, so we were ready when a lucky break through the University of Puget Sound landed us on an exchange program in muggy, beautiful, winery-free Fujian Province in 2015.

* * *

From the large windows of our guest faculty apartment at Fujian Normal University in Fuzhou, the capital of Fujian Province, the hot muggy weather and torrential summer rains reminded us that this wasn't wine country. French winemaker Gérard Colin, the Indiana Jones of wine, once had an office here. Being quite the adventurer, he'd considered starting a vineyard in the area, but even he gave up in the face of summer rain.

For once, there were no wineries to distract us. Everywhere we went in China, we got carried away by our wine plans and often missed all the key tourist sites. The only reason we walked the Great Wall was because we attended a wine trade event nearby. In Fuzhou, we promised ourselves to behave better. The number one thing to do in Fuzhou, according to locals and Trip Advisor, was to visit a refurbished historical neighborhood called San Fang Qi Xiang (Three Lanes and Seven Alleys). It had something for everyone: history, statues ready for shameless selfies,

McDonald's, Starbucks, and a dizzying variety of delicious local snacks. All this was great, but we admit we had another reason to go. Grace Vineyard, our favorite winery from Shanxi Province, had opened their own showcase restaurant in the neighborhood, thousands of miles away from their vineyards and guesthouse.

The first time we went, it was called E Yan, which could be loosely translated as "joyful banquet." Tucked in one of the alleys along a little canal, the restaurant was a haven of peace and quiet in crowded San Fang Qi Xiang. Travel and food TV shows, including Anthony Bourdain's *No Reservations*, were playing without the sound on a big screen at one end of the room, and Grace Vineyard's bottles were on display at the other. The wine list featured several Grace wines by the glass, of course, as well as wines of the world.

This is where we first met Snow, a hilarious and adorable wine professional and young mom in her late twenties, who was then the restaurant's marketing manager. After majoring in business English in college, she got into the wine trade by working at the (now-closed) Fuzhou branch of Everwines. Thanks to the shop's Grace connection, she went on to work for the winery's Fuzhou headquarters, translating communications for the marketing manager.

E Yan had been open for five years but never quite turned a good-enough profit, Snow explained. At first, it was a Chinese restaurant, offering a chef's table. The concept was that you called in advance and told them what you wanted to eat. The team then bought the ingredients and prepared your request. It turned out to be way too complicated for customers at the time. They transitioned to a more typical restaurant with Cantonese cuisine but never quite reached the success they hoped for. The E Yan we got to know served Western food, mixing fancy steakhouse with casual Spanish and Italian staples. It worked. People loved the food, and they came back, but not often enough. Too many patrons viewed E Yan as a place for a special occasion.

In addition to regulars not being as regular as they could be, E Yan didn't look like the kind of place where you would stop by for a quick bite and a drink. Dim lights, classy decor, and servers wearing black pants and white shirts made E Yan look like a place for special occasions. And yet, once you looked past this first impression, it had a more relaxed and casual side. Sure, you could splurge by ordering the eight-ounce grilled Australian Wagyu sirloin with truffle sauce. But you didn't have to, and we certainly never did. We preferred to choose from the many affordable plates, like an eighty-eight-yuan Spanish paella, a sixty-eight-yuan spaghetti carbonara, and a crème brûlée dessert for twenty-eight yuan. In casual restaurants and cafés, we often saw young Chinese friends share plates like these with a milkshake and coffee. But E Yan's high-end atmosphere didn't feel like the place for that. There was a dissonance between the two faces of E Yan that had to change.

A year after our first visit, we went back to E Yan, but only for a quick flight of Grace wines. Snow's shift was about to end, and she wanted to show us something new: their sister restaurant, Angelina. We still had fond memories of tasting Grace's experimental sparkling wine at the winery in Shanxi. They had now released not one but four bubblies, a series called Angelina after one of Judy Chan's daughters. Her other daughter, Tasya, already had a line of premium wines in her name, so Angelina was the natural inspiration. With a turquoise background and golden drawing of little Angelina holding her stuffed monkey, the bottle labels played the cute card on the three entry-level bubblies. The Chardonnay, Chenin Blanc, and Cabernet Franc were all strategically priced at 158 yuan (about twenty-three dollars), 10 yuan cheaper than Chandon's Ningxia Brut. You could buy them online and watch the animated version of Angelina and her stuffed animal or enjoy them at the winery's new restaurant in Fuzhou.

It was after nine when Snow ended her busy day, grabbed her bag, and ordered a ride on Didi, the ubiquitous Chinese taxi app. The drive was much shorter than we expected, only ten minutes from E Yan. We'd seen Angelina sparkling wine labels and recognized the signature turquoise and gold letters on the restaurant's entrance right away. The place looked nothing like E Yan. Servers wore jeans, a casual soft denim-style blue shirt with rolled-up sleeves, and a black Angelina apron. Next to a bookshelf with magazines, three empty Angelina bottles stood next to tiny action figures of famous soccer players. The side wall was black with white and blue drawings of little Angelina holding her stuffed monkey, blowing bubbles toward a tree, and playing hopscotch. "Dreams and Stories of Love" it said next to a short write-up of the story in traditional Chinese characters. With cushy chairs, couch seating along the walls, a coffeehouse-style table layout, and pop tunes filling the air, this was a comfortable, casual place and the opposite of intimidating.

Front entrance of Angelina showcasing the bottles.

Judy's father bought the space in 2003 to help set up a wine shop that could be operated without the pressure of rent, Snow explained. In February 2016, it became Angelina, the restaurant. And unlike E Yan, it quickly turned a profit. More casual and focused only on affordable plates and drinks, it attracted young people right away. Snow ordered from the late-

night menu: truffle fries, a choucroute-like dish with sausage and sauer-
kraut, and a tomato seafood pot. "It's for those born after 1988," Snow
said. "I say this because I'm 1989," she added. Behind us, four college-
aged women were busy taking selfies, each holding their own flute of
Angie cocktail, the signature house mixed drink with pineapple juice,
Blue Curaçao, and Angelina sparkling as the bubbly agent. We couldn't
resist getting one too.

The next day, we came back for a late lunch to see some daytime
action. Sunlight helping, the beauty of the location finally struck us.
Angelina was right across from the southeast entrance of a major Fuzhou
attraction, West Lake Park. On the way out of the park, pedestrians
couldn't miss Angelina's inviting bright colors and comfy chairs, since
the crosswalk from the park's entrance landed at the restaurant's door.
We got one last Angie cocktail for the road while waiting for our carbonara and paella. Snow was right about the post-1988 crowd. Here they
were, hanging out and playing on their phones. A young woman, with a
thick book as her lunch companion, ordered a salad bowl and a chocolate
cake, with a flute of Angie sparkling. She brought the flute up to her nose
several times, carefully taking in aromas, and swirled the wine in her
mouth for a bit. Like her, we forgot about time, read, and used the Wi-Fi
for a while.

Seeing the results, Grace's team renovated E Yan for a fresh reopen-
ing, as a second location of Angelina, to attract a more casual, younger,
and more regular crowd, the kind who hung out at Starbucks or Maan
Coffee a short walk away. A few months later, Grace opened the San
Fang Qi Xiang location, which meant they had a highly visible and popular bistro serving their wines in the heart of the top two tourist sites in
Fuzhou. We suspect that unlike us, many (even most) people didn't enter
Angelina because they were Grace Vineyard fans. We'd even bet that
most patrons were, at first, unaware the place belonged to one of the
country's leading wineries. They came because it looked cool, and hopefully a few would become wine fans as well after having a glass. E Yan
reopened too, but in a new location inside an upscale mall, and focused
on fine dining with dim lights, white tablecloths, and a classically trained
maître d'.

So, you see, finding our favorite Chinese wines was not such an impossible task after all. Year after year, it was getting a little easier. Still,
after all our efforts, we hadn't found a way to take home any wine by one

of our favorite local French winemakers, Gérard Colin, the Indiana Jones of wine. Two years after we first met in Xinjiang, we visited him at his new post in Shandong Province. We could have secured a steady supply of the wines he made there, if only we'd talked to our bank first. Let us show you the place first, and we'll fill you in on the details.

* * *

Gérard Colin stood out in the crowd of people waiting at arrivals in the shiny new Yantai airport. "Bonjour, ça va?" His heavy cough made us feel guilty for the ninety minutes he spent on the road with his driver just to pick us up. "I have a cold," he said without losing one bit of his cheerful mood. After his Xinjiang gig, he came back to Shandong for an extravagant wine project near the city of Rushan. The owner, who made his fortune in real estate, didn't just hire Gérard for his winemaking talent to work in the shadows. On the way to Taila, or Taiyihu as the project was called in Chinese, we couldn't miss the billboard on the freeway, with Gérard, larger than life, smiling and offering a bunch of grapes in his hands. The same picture greeted us in the driveway entrance around the fountain, printed on the full length of an impressive four-by-four limousine. And in case we didn't get the idea yet, many bottle labels featured a portrait of the "Lafite Master," as several brochures called him, to play up his previous association with the Lafite project near Penglai. We were almost disappointed not to find his statue on the property. In Xinjiang, remember, he was roughing it, Indiana Jones style. But at Taila, he lived like James Bond, in a comfortable suite on the ground floor of the main building, Chateau 007. And even James Bond couldn't brag that he had an office in Chateau Margaux, a full-size French-style castle, a five-minute bike ride away through the vines, named in homage to the top Bordeaux winery.

With Gérard on board, Taila's 2014 Chardonnay won a gold medal at the Concours Mondial de Bruxelles. A year later, the rosé of Cabernet Franc snatched a silver medal. From dry whites, unoaked or aged in oak, to red blends and sweet wines, Gérard worked with the terroir and his wealth of wine imagination to produce a wide range of styles. He had a fond memory of an evening at a fancy hotel in New York a long time ago, when he bought himself takeout pizza and picked up a bottle of blush rosé that gave him so much joy that a recipe for it brewed in his mind for years. That was the inspiration for his off-dry rosé at Taila. For one of the dessert wines, he used Italian Riesling grapes that had been affected by Botrytis, a noble kind of rot that, under the right conditions and in the right hands, concentrates the juice into shriveled grapes and makes luscious sweet wines. When they saw the fungus in the vineyard, Chinese colleagues got ready to throw the bunches away. But no, Gérard explained, a lucky wonderful thing had just happened, and he had to take advantage of it. They thought he was crazy. But the boss trusted him with the winemaking, and he enjoyed a lot of freedom to follow his inspiration. And the wine was delicious.

So where could consumers buy the wines? With Gérard's fame and the medals, did a distributor get on board? Maybe a restaurant or two in Beijing? "We don't sell wine," Gérard explained. Really? That was the fun fact about Taila wines: they were not on the market. Oh, sure, there were price tags on the bottles at the winery and visitors could buy some there. But the core business lay elsewhere. Taila's wines were for members only.

Now, wine enthusiasts in the United States are familiar with the concept of a wine club. Some wineries invite you to commit to a certain quantity of wine over the calendar year, holding your credit card number as a guarantee. And in exchange, you get better deals, access to exclusive members-only releases, and parties at the estate. Taila took the idea much further. You could call it a wine country club. To become a Taila investor, people paid a one-time startup investment to rent a chunk of vineyard for ten years. For fifteen thousand yuan, an investor got one-tenth of a mu and an allocation of sixty bottles per year at the preferential price of ninety-nine yuan per bottle. The seventy-five-thousand-yuan plan included five times as much vineyard area and three hundred bottles per year at sixty-three yuan each. The high prices (in the hundreds) listed for the wines made the members-only fee per bottle look like a bargain. Moreover, members got that extra special feeling from having wines that outsiders couldn't have. To make investors feel like true VIPs, there were other perks, of course. They could bring family and friends to enjoy "their" wine at the resort. Every tenth of a mu investment gave access to ten nights per year, at the rate of ninety-nine yuan, a bargain compared to the nonmember listed rate of 580 yuan. They could stay in one of the hotel suites or, even better, a cottage in the middle of the vineyard. And they were invited to annual events such as the harvest festival, a golf tournament, and a beauty pageant.

The swimming and boating activities we saw in promotional videos were off the menu when we visited, unfortunately. The "no deep-water swimming" signs stood oddly in a bunch of bushes quite far from the water, due to the lake drying up by half over the previous two years. But there were other ways to enjoy the property. Cynthia put on her running gear to explore the grounds and compensate for the eating and drinking to come. Following the path along the vines down from our cottage to the lake, she jogged by farmers on duty in the vineyard and at the organic vegetable garden, stopped to admire cute animals at the petting zoo, wondered if anyone had ever used the helicopter parking lot, and waved to the boss who gave her words of encouragement. Meanwhile, Pierre took an easy walk to the wedding chapel, complete with kissing swans in a heart shape by the lake. And he almost got hit by a golf ball as he watched a happy family of investors practice their swing at the driving range.

Even without spending the night, just stopping by to pick up your allocated wine was more thrilling than going to a wine shop. One afternoon at the front desk, a middle-aged woman came to pick up a few bottles wrapped in a classy wooden box with Gérard's signature on it. Imagine her delight when the Lafite Master himself came to greet her. Much laughter ensued on the way to her car as Gérard kept offering to carry the box and she repeatedly refused. "They're investors from Beijing. Very nice people," Gérard said after she left. Building relationships, giving people stories to go with their wine—that was also part of his role here. That night, at dinner, he traded his shorts and T-shirt for dress pants and a sleek black Mao shirt. He was on call. Investors were spending the night, which meant honoring many requests for *ganbei* toasts at Chateau 007 with their own private French winemaker. Most foreigners traveling to China for business fear *ganbei* (literally, dry cup), an important part of Chinese drinking culture. But Gérard liked *ganbei*. "It's a culture of sharing," he said. He finds it warm and genuine, a good time with friends who enjoy each other's company, and a welcome contrast to what he saw as the "culture of appearance" of intellectualized wine tastings.

Did Taila's approach work? It looked like it. While many Chinese wineries struggled to find their market, Taila was selling everything easily. Large up-front payments and ten-year commitments made finances more predictable. By August 2016, there were one thousand investors, with an average commitment of one-tenth of mu, the basic plan. With the thirty-thousand-mu estate, including 90 percent devoted to vines, there was room for a lot of investors. A few were invited to dream bigger. Tired of staying in the little cottage? Huge chateaux under construction punctuated the vineyard, ready to be claimed by ambitious new VIPs. In the meantime, a new project had just started: seminars for amateur home winemakers. Gérard said there were hundreds of them in big cities, people who bought grapes from the best wine regions, including Ningxia. Here at Taila, they could learn from the "Lafite Master" himself, using grapes from the estate. Yet another way to make sure no drop went unsold.

We admit we had mixed feelings about the Taila model. It was exciting that the wines were good and attracted investors. But with wines only accessible to a lucky few, what good would it do for Chinese wine more broadly? We weren't sure. Before we left, Gérard kindly gave us two bottles to take home. Alas, since we hadn't talked to our bank ahead of time, we didn't take the plunge and become investors. That meant no steady supply of Taila wines for us. Fortunately, by then, we finally had several go-to places to fill our wine suitcase with some good variety. Still, wouldn't it be nice to just run into the Chinese wines we love, no planning required, and just order a glass? It finally happened when we least expected it.

One of several Taila chateaux ready to be claimed by an ambitious investor.

* * *

We had just waved goodbye to our three-month-old niece, Isabelle, in Ho Chi Minh City. From there, our clearest path to Ningxia was a straight flight to Guangzhou, a night at the airport hotel, and an early morning flight to Yinchuan. We checked in late at the Pullman Guangzhou Airport Hotel, tired but hungry. In this kind of situation, Cynthia usually needs some sort of creamy Italian pasta dish, while Pierre's thoughts are set on noodle soup. Our best bet that night was the eclectic hotel restaurant that offered everything from Western food and pan-Asian dishes to sushi and Japanese steakhouse staples. Wine was nowhere on our agenda. So, imagine our surprise when we saw Kanaan wines available by the glass. At last, we had just *run into* one of our favorite wineries. We shared a dry Riesling and the Pretty Pony red blend, perfect pairings with a layover en route for Yinchuan. They even had Chandon's Ningxia sparkling wines. We finally had a sign that with every trip, there would be even more places for people to try our favorite Chinese wines.

In fact, a year later, we ran into more wines we expected even less: Gérard Colin's wines from Puchang Winery in Xinjiang. They were on the menu, by the glass, at Green, the restaurant in the lobby of Hotel ICON, in Hong Kong. We even found a few bottles at a local wine shop, Enoteca. In Beijing, we enjoyed excellent Ningxia wines at a new restaurant called The Merchants and were pleased to see Grace Vineyard and 1421 by the glass at the Novotel. With the big brands like Changyu and Great Wall improving their game—who knows, supermarkets in the mainland may soon become a good source too. But what if you didn't plan to go to China anytime soon? People frequently ask us which wineries export and where they can find them. That's the subject of the next chapter.

11

COMING TO AMERICA

"Check your office mailbox before you go home tonight. I stumbled on something interesting today and bought one for you and one for us." The cryptic email from Mike Veseth, of *Wine Economist* fame, sent Pierre running.

"Cyn! Look at this," he shouted from the entryway.

"Niiiiice! Where did it come from?"

Somehow, on a slight lunch detour from an IKEA shopping trip in 2014, Mike and his wife Sue had found a bottle of Changyu wine. Yes, you know, the giant, state-owned winery with the 4-D movie theater in the Italian castle? This one was from Shandong, the label said, and the vintage was, well, surprising: "2003," we read, eyes crinkling, simultaneously elated and wary. Really? We had to try it right away, and it wasn't good. Not at all. But for us, it was about more than just taste. Smell and taste are like a zipline to the hippocampus, taking you straight back to old memories. This wine felt so familiar and strangely, viscerally fun. A familiar streak of odd and green, unripe aromas flew out of the glass, taking us right back to the cellar at the Changyu Wine Culture Museum in Yantai, where the red wine samples tasted just like this during our first visit.

A few days later, we drove to the Great Wall Shopping Mall, close to IKEA in Kent, Washington, where Mike and Sue's present came from. And here it was, Changyu Cabernet Dry Red, 2003, standing next to the Yellow Tail Reserve, on top of the freezer, overlooking a wide array of frozen dumplings. It made it here thanks to Co-Ho Imports, a company that imports Asian wines and spirits for distribution in Washington and Oregon,[1] although the 2000 and 2003 Changyu Cabernets were the only two grape wines on the list. By now, Changyu has made so much more and better wine that it's amazing anyone here would still be carrying these, particularly at the eyebrow-raising eighteen-dollar price tag.

As much as we enjoyed the tasting experiment, we knew that the Changyu 2003 Cabernet would not lead the global Chinese wine break-through we were waiting for. Neither would a couple of old bottles we found at a Chinatown liquor store in San Francisco. You can imagine our surprise in 2015 when we received an intriguing interview request from a New York–based reporter for the *China Daily*. His editor charged him with exploring "the growing trend of Chinese wines in the US market." Really? Had we missed something big? Did *China Daily* have a serious scoop? We did get our hopes up and looked forward to our phone conver-sation. When the question came up, we replied based on what we knew: "As far as we know, while you can find an odd bottle here or there, it's not really a trend. But what have you found?" We were dying to be proven wrong. His reaction ended our brief period of hope: "Oh, wow, if you guys say that too . . ." Alas, that's what he'd heard from several authorities on Chinese wine. But we told him there was something to the idea.

After all, so much had changed since that first year when we obses-sively scoured wine lists and blogs for new places to find Chinese wines. Back then, Pierre watched with concern and disbelief as Cynthia stuffed as many bottles as she could in cheap travel bags found at a Beijing supermarket, protecting them with a combination of clothes and bubble wrap. Miraculously, all the bottles survived, but we fantasized about recommending Chinese wines our friends could actually buy. Occasional-ly, we found projects that seemed too good to be true. And in the end, we learned that just as in most of life, those things would turn out to be pieces of the story rather than miracles. We'd obsessively followed "Mid-dle Kingdom Wines," the website of a UK company planning to import several of our favorite wines, but no stores were ever announced and the site eventually disappeared. The American counterpart of that case study came in 2013, just three months after our first visit, when we learned we could get Ningxia wine samples shipped to our house from a guy in Texas. We had never tried it, but what if it was the kind of wine we needed? The kind that would help us blow people's mind about how good Chinese wine could be?

* * *

"Well, at first we called it 'Chinese' wine, but that was a mistake. If you want to call it Chinese wine, it would have to be one of the twenty-six indigenous grapes, or be plum wine or rice wine," David Henderson, owner of China Fine Wines, explained. "We produce wine made in China, but all of our vines are from Bordeaux," he insisted. Back in the late 1990s, when he first spotted vineyards he could work with in Ningxia, David already knew a thing or two about the potential of wine in China. Ten years earlier, he founded Montrose Food and Wine, the first company in the country to be licensed as a direct importer of wine, representing big names like Robert Mondavi and Kendall Jackson. In 2007, he moved on to an ambitious project: making a line of Ningxia wines for export to the United States. He called it Dragon's Hollow, a name that foreigners could easily associate with the Middle Kingdom. It was an uphill battle from the start: "We made a mistake because of people's prejudice, so that was our first hurdle. If we say Chinese wine, people think it will be disgusting." But by 2013, he felt change coming. With improvements in the wine and packaging, and positive feedback at tastings, he eventually placed Dragon's Hollow in a few places, including a high-end Chinese restaurant in Las Vegas. One of Pierre's students spotted Dragon's Hollow at Total Wine and More in Reno. Who would have thought?

David proved that despite a wall of skepticism, introducing respectable Chinese wine in the United States was possible after all. The reasonable price point—twelve dollars—helped bring a few buyers on board. In May 2014, when we were invited to give a keynote presentation for an Asian studies lecture series at the University of Washington Tacoma, and needed enough wine to entertain the audience, our own basement stash of Grace Vineyard and the like was too small. We naturally turned to Dragon's Hollow, the only ones we could get in sufficient quantity for an event like this, shipped from China Fine Wines's Texas office.

At our UW Tacoma evening, we knew it had to be a blind tasting next to similarly priced wines from established regions, or China wouldn't stand a chance. Scores of researchers, from economists to sensory scientists, have demonstrated how biased wine tasters, pros and novices alike, can be. Anything you know about a wine can affect your appreciation.

And guess what? The audience preferred Dragon's Hollow to an Australian Chardonnay at the same price. On the Cabernet Sauvignon, attendees' preferences split about half and half next to a red Bordeaux. Was Dragon's Hollow amazing wine? No, and to be honest, our hearts go to other producers. But that night in Tacoma, our guests, including some Chinese students and professors who had never tasted wine made in their motherland, were genuinely pleased. We had to play this game again, but with a more demanding audience.

Our Chinese wines safely packed in the trunk, we drove south to Portland, Oregon, to the Wine and Spirits Archive. It's one of those little wine schools that offers a variety of fun tasting classes and formal certifications up to the advanced level of Wine and Spirit Education Trust (WSET). We had met Mimi, owner and lead wine instructor, a few months earlier, when we spent a couple of weekends taking one of her WSET courses. She had never tried Chinese wines, and neither had her regulars.

We were nervous. Without realizing it, we had scheduled our Portland outing at a special time for Americans: Super Bowl 2015 (when many Portlanders temporarily became Seattleites). Adding to our fears, a few of the bottles opened before the guests arrived turned out to be out of condition and smelled off, forcing us to switch to potentially less exciting backup options. And if anybody showed up at all, we knew we'd face a much tougher group this time. Unlike at the UW event, where most attendees were new to wine and eager to drink at a research talk, here we would face seasoned wine enthusiasts.

Perhaps the biggest surprise of the day was that somehow Mimi managed to sell out all seats for our guest lecture. Few people believed it would happen, and yet, that afternoon, eighteen Portlanders skipped the Super Bowl and came to a blind tasting of wines made in China instead. Students, including China travelers, wine professionals, and a tea expert, were cheerful as they grabbed their welcome bubbly and took their seats. They were genuinely excited to taste Chinese wine for the first time and learn about the emerging local industry. The blind tasting included Dragon's Hollow (delivered from Texas) and a few other Chinese wines we'd managed to protect in our basement. Mimi threw a Chilean Cabernet Sauvignon and a white Burgundy into the lineup to add some suspense and keep tasters guessing. Even experienced tasters can be tricked at blind tastings. Would we manage to make them admit that Chinese wine is delicious?

"Yeah . . . it's OK . . ." one attendee commented on one wine. "Passable," a guy in the back said of another. There was unanimous praise for one Chardonnay in the lineup, but it was the white Burgundy. "I think it's interesting. You know, I would serve it to show something different," another one said about Dragon's Hollow Chardonnay after it was revealed. It turned out to be the class favorite among Chinese whites, but it couldn't compete with the Burgundy. However, on the reds, Dragon's Hollow Cabernet Sauvignon got first place, ahead of not only its Chinese comrades but also a Chilean Cab at the same price point. "The quality is good on these wines," Mimi told us after the tasting. People had fun, Chinese wine was now on their radar, and they found it of "acceptable" quality (an official WSET standard). But we had yet to really impress them. Not a bad outcome, of course. But the kind of "aha" moments we were hoping for didn't happen. If only we could show them our favorite wines.

Maybe we could get new and improved Dragon's Hollow wines from David and come back for a rematch? We couldn't fly to Beijing every time we needed a Chinese wine refill. We hoped David's adventure would continue, soaking in all the progress in Ningxia winemaking and viticulture of the last few years, so we'd have at least one source at home. Unfortunately, last time we talked, it didn't seem likely. Despite the good feedback, clients weren't coming back for more. It was just too hard, and David sounded ready to move on, although he said he would jump back in if the opportunity presented itself. If that bottle in the Reno store ever sold, it probably wasn't replaced.

In 2015, we'd started to accept the idea that the trusty Wine Check luggage case we'd found would have to do. But then a shopping trip in Hong Kong gave us new hope.

* * *

Waiting at Fuzhou airport for our flight to board, panic struck: "Oh my gosh, we forgot to plan where to eat in Hong Kong this afternoon!" Fortunately, the solution sat in video form on our tablet. So there we were, at our boarding gate, sharing a pair of headphones, notebooks in hand, cramming our homework with the Hong Kong episode of our new favorite TV show: *The Flying Winemaker*.

You may not know Eddie McDougall, aka The Flying Winemaker, but avid readers of wine business news may remember his intriguing project. A Canadian woman had the eccentric idea of starting an urban winery in Hong Kong, making wine with flash-frozen grapes imported from Washington State.[2] It turns out Eddie was one of her winemakers. Half Chinese, born in Hong Kong and raised in Australia, Eddie fell into wine after graduating with a business degree and not being quite sure where to go from there. While working at a fine-dining restaurant in Australia, a leftover pour of Alsace Pinot Blanc crossed his lips, leading to, as he put it, a moment of clarity. He enrolled in a wine science program, and the rest is history. In a few years, he established The Flying Winemaker as a multifaceted business.

In the middle of an office building in central Hong Kong, even the coolest of businesses are not always easy to find. The crammed little shop, company headquarters, tiny wine warehouse, and wine education classroom were packed with cases of wines of the world. We assumed at best we would find the Chinese wines we needed to reach our luggage limit, but it turned out to be much more interesting. Next to their Chinese counterparts, we found cases of Thai, Balinese, Indian, Japanese, and Malaysian wine, as well as several people who obviously shared our passion for innovation in emerging wine regions.

The Flying Winemaker had just started the *Asian Wine Review*, a neat little book with an overview of Asian wine-growing areas and producers, complete with point ratings established through blind tastings. It's their blue ocean project, Eddie explained, using a popular business term for strategies aiming to find market niches with little existing competition. He admitted it wasn't an easy sale, having met his share of travelers fresh from a revolting experience with local wine on a Bali vacation, and who swore they would never let that happen again. We can relate, as this is a common reaction when people learn about our research. But like us, Eddie and his team believe that emerging wine regions will bring a more diverse and more exciting wine world. When it happens, they want to be among those who helped to tell the story. But who's the market, we asked? For Eddie, an important part of it is Asian millennials, increasingly conscious about where their food comes from and getting into craft beer. The TV show tries to convince them the good stuff is at their doorstep. Don't just go to Thailand for pad thai and coconuts, he suggests. Looking for a wine adventure? Bordeaux and Napa are so far away.

How about a regional flight to the Thai wine tourism trail? Watch the Thailand episode of *The Flying Winemaker* and you'll see what he means.

The show, which aired on Australian public television, Discovery Channel Asia Pacific, and on twenty airlines, adds visibility to the shop and promotes Eddie's idea of wine as something cool, fun, and not confined to white-tablecloth restaurants. A good illustration is a project called the "Rosé Revolution," which started in 2011 as a party where two hundred guests tasted a dozen rosés from various places. It was so successful that it prompted the opening of the shop, and Eddie expanded Rosé Revolution events in several Asian cities with more than fifty wineries. When you watch the show, count the number of times Eddie expresses his love of rosé. He sees it as an approachable wine category, suitable for special wine-pairing dinners as well as pool parties, and one that perhaps could help get more Asians into wine.

Can Eddie's idea of wine help promote Chinese wine? The China chapter of the *Asian Wine Review* is a good start. Just look at the comments on some of the wines we encountered earlier in this book:

> Grace Vineyard's Angelina Sparkling gets a bronze medal and 87 points: "A gentle stream of minerality and good acidity keep the wine energetic and lively."
> Kanaan's Pretty Pony 2013 takes a gold medal with 93 points: "A wine with a beautiful core of blackberries and ripe plums. . . . This is a wine that is purposely built for the future and those serious about Cabernet Sauvignon."
> Silver Heights's "The Summit" 2013 earns Best Trophy at 97 points and a tasting note that concludes, "Magic."

These were a far cry from the old tasting notes with "hints of urinal crust" and "baked dead mouse" from earlier years. Could people like Eddie pick up where others had left off? In the meantime, our wine suitcase was complete with the latest Chinese wines we loved, a couple of other Asian wines we'd never tried, and a copy of the *Asian Wine Review* to dream about future wine field trips.

* * *

We came back to Mimi's little school in Portland a year later for a rematch, with new wines from our latest checked luggage bounty. This time, even the welcome bubbly was Chinese: the Chandon rosé from

Ningxia. Students, some of them back from the year before, played the guessing game, knowing there would be one to two non-Chinese wines in the lineup. The white wines performed well, and one taster, before the Ningxia Jiabeilan rosé was revealed, speculated it could be from Provence. But the real breakthrough came next.

"This cannot be Chinese!" one guy exclaimed, implying that the second blind red must be Italian. "Or they have come a *really* long way [since last year's tasting]." The wine was Grace Vineyard's Aglianico from Shanxi Province, but we weren't going to tell them right away. Ha, it was happening, at last! We understood what journalist George Taber must have felt when he covered the Judgment of Paris in 1976, the famous blind tasting where Napa wines won over the best Bordeaux and Burgundy with a panel of French judges. Unlike the judges, he knew what they were tasting and watched them rave about California wines with comments such as "Ah, back to France," and berate some French wines with "This must be California, it has no nose."

We tried hard to keep a straight face for as long as we could, since just before the Grace, Mimi had poured an Italian Aglianico she picked as a comparison. With brown paper bags still on the bottles, more discussion ensued. They didn't just like the Chinese one; they preferred it. At the big reveal, people were impressed. And unlike the Paris judges in George Taber's story, they didn't try to take their words back.

Moving on to the third red, tasters seemed intensely focused on figuring it out. Glass in hand, the same guy who'd spoken up on the Grace Aglianico admitted that he was taking his time; since we had just fooled him, he wasn't sure what to think anymore. The third red was Grace Vineyard's Marselan, a grape variety that none of them, not even Mimi, had ever had as a single varietal red. And the fourth was Jiabeilan's white label red blend. Finally, we had led a tasting where a group of seasoned wine enthusiasts, even some with WSET credentials and who work in the business, could find Chinese wines genuinely enjoyable, not as a curiosity but because they were high-quality wines that tasted good. Now if only they could find them in stores.

* * *

Our friend Mike faked a heart attack when Cynthia revealed the red wine we opened for dinner. Earlier that day, Pierre had set aside a delicious

Languedoc red from the Faugères appellation. But when Cynthia got home, she suggested that, instead, maybe it was time to open *that* bottle.

It had started two months earlier, when Pierre had to make the traffic-ridden drive from Tacoma up to Bellevue to vote in the final round of the French presidential election. With Emmanuel Macron on one side and Marine Le Pen on the other, every ballot mattered more than ever, many journalists urged. But French voting is, in practice, ridiculously simple, and after over an hour's drive, Pierre's civic duty took three minutes. So, he had to make other plans to increase the fun-to-drive ratio. With his ballot cast, he drove to the nearest Total Wine and More.

It was the first time that either of us had to ask for staff assistance to open the special wine fridge. Pierre stood in front of it, almost with stage fright. Five feet to the right, at eye level, were several vintages of Chateau Margaux and other top-flight Bordeaux, the kind that sometimes went for astonishing prices at Hong Kong auctions. On the left, closer to our target, there was the Cote Bonneville DuBrul Vineyard red, one of Washington's top wines, many times less expensive than most of its competitors in the fridge, but still a hefty 120 dollars. We'd enjoyed it once at a trade tasting, for free, and agreed that we would never pay this much money for a bottle of wine, ever.

But this time was different, and the French election was a great cover for our real agenda of the day. As the cashier scanned the bottle at the register, she looked at Pierre and said, "That will be $329.99 please. Can I see your ID?"

It turns out a lot goes in your head when you walk back to the car holding that one bottle in its glorious brown paper bag. "What if I trip and break it? What if a Canada goose gang flies by and takes it away?" Once safely seated in our little Toyota Yaris, Pierre blasted the air-conditioning at feet level in the passenger seat to re-create some semblance of temperature control on this screaming hot day. A couple of hours later, Ao Yun, Moët Hennessy's wine from the high mountains of Yunnan near Shangri-la, took its spot on our basement wine rack. Boy, when they said it would be expensive, they weren't kidding.

Moët Hennessy had always planned a release of this first vintage in Europe and the United States, in addition to the Chinese market. We assumed we'd read about it in a wine magazine, and that it would never ever touch our lips. And remember, the boss never invited us. It was person-to-person fieldwork that took us to the little guesthouse in Adong village that just happened to be the staff dorm and the home of one of Moët's grape farmers. People were nice to hang out with us after work, but they stayed professional and followed orders. We never saw the inside of the winery, nor was there any secret lab sample smuggled out of the building for us to try. What is more, surely, as soon as it came out in the US, we thought, every collector would scoop up the handful of bottles available at each location well before we could even begin to convince ourselves to pay for it. But the wine had been at Total Wine and More in Bellevue for a few months, and based on the store's records (we had to ask), we bought only the second bottle out of seventy or so left in stock. This was not a top-secret impossible-to-find wine after all.

Two months later, as we prepared for dinner, we learned that Mike and Sue had just celebrated their forty-first anniversary. And Mike had written about Ao Yun in his new book, *Around the World in Eighty Wines*, admitting to his readers that unfortunately, he'd never tasted it. Cynthia had caught the perfect moment to finally open *that* bottle. And we learned something else about spending this kind of money on wine when the time came to put a corkscrew in it. We got nervous: "Please don't be corked, please don't be corked." Cork taint is the terrible chemical problem affecting about 4 percent of wine bottles and one of the biggest reasons servers in restaurants allow you a small taste when you order a bottle. The dreaded TCA compound tends to contaminate corks, making beautiful wine smell like wet cardboard or other awfulness.

Cynthia kept trying to reassure Pierre that "if it's corked, it'll still make a great story and we'll take the bottle back." Yeah, right. But phew. Bright aromas of black currant jumped off the freshly opened bottle. At dinner, it was as delicious as we'd hoped. And we say this as people who are easily disappointed by this sort of elite wine experience. Many people ask us, "Is it worth over three hundred bucks?" Well, if you calculate a taste-to-price ratio and compare it to the amazing wines you could try for a tenth the price, of course not. But we're almost certain we enjoyed it more than any other excellent, insanely expensive wine we could have bought. You see, taste is a complicated thing. We had so many great memories and friends associated with this wine, as we relived our Yunnan adventures with truly outstanding wine.

Is Ao Yun a good ambassador for Chinese wine in the US and Europe? Maybe, if all the sector needs to break through outside of the motherland is a ridiculously high-end brand leader. But we're not so sure.

Look at Moët Hennessy's stories of their work in China. Mid-range sparkling wine in Ningxia—sure, they can make lots of that for the Chinese market and help build the local market for bubbles. But for a top red? No, Ningxia was apparently not good enough for them. They just had to go all the way up the mountains of Yunnan, many hours of a scary drive away from the nearest airport. They had to cherry-pick a handful of villages, and unlike Lafite in Shandong Province, they didn't settle around Adong because it would be convenient. What do we learn from Ao Yun's story? That to make it, Moët had to do the impossible. And drinking the impossible—well, that will be $329.99, please. How many people, anywhere, are really going to taste this? If a brand is going to put Chinese wine on many dinner tables worldwide, it's probably not going to be Ao Yun. So, who else?

* * *

Cynthia had one of those sushi cravings that always take us to H Mart, the Asian grocery store where we can find the fresh fish and supplies she needs to make it at home for a fraction of a restaurant bill. But this time, we learned something new.

Before heading to the fish section, we browsed through the wine wall, as we always do just in case we learn something that inspires our writing or our taste buds. "Wow, look at that! It's Changyu Moser 2013!" We couldn't believe it. Here it was, on sale for eighteen dollars. Oh, Changyu, the fond memories we have built together. When it came to tourism, from our first Italian castle to the 4-D movie theater, we loved it all. But the wines? Well, so far it had been hit or miss. We'd heard good and bad things about this 2013 Cabernet Sauvignon. Berry and Rudd, the famous London fine wine merchant, seems able to sell it, and Eddie The Flying Winemaker even called it "a good drop" on the Ningxia episode of his TV show.

We bought a bottle, of course, but it took weeks for us to open it. A friend had tried it, saying it tasted OK but a bit off balance, with clumsy oak treatment. Sigh. After delaying some more, it was on a weeknight that we went down to our basement and finally picked it up. Pierre got his Changyu stuffed animal out for encouragement and put on the winery T-shirt. Time to pop the cork and pour, armed with our lowest expectations.

Big surprise: it tasted good. Nothing extraordinary, but a nice medium-bodied Cab with some tannin, fruity with a faint herbaceous note.

No clumsy oak, no weird anything. A perfectly enjoyable weeknight red. We're not sure what's going on with tasters' mixed experience with this wine. Are there major inconsistencies in this bottling? Are some bottles out of condition due to poor storage and transport?

We're especially hopeful about this because Changyu's 2015 Moser family red is out on the world market too. We haven't found it here yet, but we know it is sold in stores in the UK, and all the reviews we have seen are very good. In fact, as of 2019, a new specialist importer of Chinese wines, Panda Fine Wines, was operating in the UK, with a small but exciting portfolio. Changyu has also started to place more wine in European supermarkets. One of Changyu's brands, Noble Dragon, is available in various supermarkets and wine stores not only in the UK but also in Spain, Germany, Switzerland, and Russia.

There is so much more to Chinese wine than Changyu, of course. Hopefully, others will follow. But we get that only a megabrand like this was powerful enough to place Chinese wine on supermarket shelves where everyone could see it. We'll buy it again and look hard for that promising 2015 too.

All this made us quite jealous of the UK market, Brexit notwithstanding. So, imagine our delight when, thanks to having finally started an Instagram account, we learned about an exciting opportunity close to home: a 2019 Chinese New Year dinner in Portland, featuring all Chinese wines. The wines were from Shanxi Province, by Chateau Rongzi, a neighbor of Grace Vineyard. We loved the wines and were happy to see that fellow dinner guests, who had never had Chinese wine, enjoyed them too. But best of all: we can buy them online from the importer, Royal Comfort Distributors, a game changer for us.

But wait, there's more. Living in Tacoma, our favorite weekend getaway is in Vancouver, Canada. And right around the corner from our favorite dim sum restaurant, the liquor store now sells—you guessed it—Chinese wine. And not just any Chinese wines: two labels from Silver Heights in Ningxia. So, yes, it looks as if Chinese wine has come to the American continent after all.

12

WHAT'S NEXT?

One morning in June 2016, a crowd of wine economists walked through the entrance of Bordeaux's new modern wine museum, the Cité du Vin. Since we started our China wine adventure, one of the perks has been presenting at the annual conference of the American Association of Wine Economists, which always combines a rigorous academic program with touring in a wine region. The 2016 edition gave us the chance to do some Bordeaux wine tourism. We'd lived in Bordeaux in 2005 while Cynthia was in graduate school at Sciences Po, the same year Yanzhi was studying enology in the building next door.

We greatly enjoyed the Cité du Vin, filled with multisensory activities, such as sitting at a virtual dinner table with headshot videos of wine celebrities (each in their own chair) engaging in exciting conversation. There was a 3-D globe movie theater, playing an anime about wine transportation through the ages. You know how much we liked these kinds of bells and whistles at Changyu castles in China. We then went upstairs to the tasting bar, which served wines from all around the world. Among the dozens of bottles on display on the bar, each wearing its country's flag, one immediately stood out to us. A simple label, thick red lines on white background: it was Yanzhi's first Ningxia wine, from Guanlan Vineyard, where we least expected it. Now a decade after Yanzhi's student days, his bottles were among the Chinese wines on rotation in the tasting room. While we waited for our turn, a couple of visitors asked the knowledgeable staff about it. "They use Bordeaux varieties, but this has a different style, with spicy notes," she explained. Chinese wine was taken seriously, and enjoyed, at Bordeaux's flagship wine museum. It made our day. And now you know one more place to have a glass of good Chinese wine.

How was Yanzhi doing, we wondered as we savored our tasting pours of Ningxia and Croatia? We hadn't crossed paths since our visit to Guanlan Vineyard and its baby vines at the foot of Helan Mountain. We knew the story behind that experimental bottle on display at Cité du Vin. The grapes still had to be bought in, and the wine was made in other wineries that Yanzhi and his young colleague, Liao, convinced to rent them some space. Was Guanlan finally under construction? We'd kept in touch through WeChat and knew Guanlan's own first crop was about to be harvested, but neither Yanzhi's nor Liao's posts indicated any progress on building the winery.

Meanwhile, Chinese wine had come a long way. Although most curious drinkers still had to go to China to enjoy it, good—even great—Chinese wine was now officially a thing. We say "officially" because wine lovers worldwide could now read all about it in major wine reference books, from the *World Atlas of Wine* by Hugh Johnson and Jancis Robinson, to Karen McNeil's popular *Wine Bible*, whose latest edition had nine pages on China. Eric Asimov, the *New York Times* wine columnist, wrote a piece complete with tasting notes. In the UK, author Janet Wang published a book, *The Chinese Wine Renaissance*, and poured Chinese wines on Channel 4's *Sunday Brunch* ahead of the 2019 Chinese New Year. Even the *Lonely Planet China* travel guide now had a full page on wine in the Ningxia chapter. When we bought our first *Lonely Planet China* in 2013, the only reference to grape wine was a short paragraph on the Changyu wine museum in Yantai.

Beyond good drinks, we wondered if all this recognition would help Chinese wine deliver what drew us to wine, and China, in the first place: the potential for the industry to promote economic development. To us, this meant opportunity for the poor, not just prestige and money for wealthy winery owners. A recent big wine conference in the south of Ningxia gave us some hope that these goals were still on the agenda.

* * *

When in 2017 Pierre received an invitation from Li Hua's College of Enology to attend the Tenth International Symposium on Viticulture and Enology, in Wuzhong, an hour south of Yinchuan, we thought we knew what it would be like. We'd been at our share of academic conferences.

The keynote speeches, given by VIPs, would be in a large lecture hall. Around that, we imagined dozens of parallel sessions spread over many small hotel meeting rooms, a little projector for PowerPoint presentations that may or may not work, and maybe six people showing up at Pierre's presentation. We were wrong.

All presentations took place in one very large room of the conference hotel, in front of a crowd of hundreds, under big lights, with professional photographers clicking away and camera crews capturing every minute. The audience was mostly composed of Chinese wine industry folks, including top winemakers, scientists, marketers, and journalists. A few government officials were there too, such as the head of Ningxia's wine bureau. The two dozen foreign guest speakers were interspersed throughout the program, and simultaneous translation was provided for all presentations through headphones.

The presentations, covering a wide range of subjects, were enlightening. But perhaps the most intriguing part of the conference happened during the breaks, and then on wine touring day. Being in Ningxia, the conference could have taken place in Yinchuan, close to the wineries we showed you earlier in this book. But the organizers' plan wasn't merely to promote Ningxia wine. They focused on those made further south in the region. We had never been to any of the wineries that had come to show their wines during breaks around the conference room. They were all from around Wuzhong and Qingtongxia, or even further south, from a district called Hongsibu.

In the early 1980s, the regional government of Ningxia developed new strategies to help people from the mountainous south of the province, who lived in poverty and drought, far from the path of the Yellow River, with little access to resources to sustain themselves beyond subsistence. Instead of trying to assist them where they were, far from everything, the government started relocating them closer to the river, building housing, and installing irrigation systems so they could engage in more productive agriculture. Moreover, it would give them a chance to get nonfarm, higher-paying jobs as the urban centers developed.[1]

Hongsibu was one of the destination spots chosen for the relocation program. Not that there was much there, but proximity to the Yellow River allowed the government to launch a major irrigation project there in 1996, along with housing development. By 2000, more than fifty thousand people, from Hui Muslim and Han communities in the drought-stricken south, had been resettled in Hongsibu. In 2017, more than two hundred thousand people lived there.

With the wine boom, the district was also betting on wine, and wine tourism of course, to boost economic development. And the conference was used as a platform to show how serious they were. The Hongsibu wines presented at an evening tasting were very good, and very different from other Ningxia wines we knew further north. After a district official in a three-piece suit gave a speech about the strengths of the area for wine and tourism and showed a promotional video, Professor Li Hua, wearing jeans and a red T-shirt, took the stage. "We just heard about the strengths of Hongsibu. So, I am going to focus on disadvantages," he said with a smile. He explained the challenge of drought and harsh winters, and the importance of having a serious agriculture strategy, "if we want our grapes to reflect our terroir." His speech was a strong reminder to all players present, from a leading authority figure, that good wine always starts in the vineyard, and that farming, farmers, and natural resources like water needed to be taken seriously and not as an afterthought next to the pretty chateau and oak barrels.

So, Ningxia officials still talked about wine as a tool for economic development. It was good to hear, but time will tell whether this remains key to the agenda in Ningxia and elsewhere. Chinese wine, which started on the better-off east coast (and continued to grow there), had now spread west to poorer regions, such as Ningxia, Yunnan, Shanxi, Shaanxi, or Xinjiang. And while we haven't been to Sichuan yet, there's a growing wine area there too. In the Northeast, provinces like Jilin and Heilong-jiang were building a reputation for quality ice wine.

Time will tell whether the fast development of the industry is sustain-able, and how benefits will be shared. Will wine bring more secured livelihoods to farmers, and the poor more generally? Will it create new, better jobs in the hospitality business? Will resources, especially water, be managed in a sustainable manner? Winemakers strive to grow the best grapes, make the best possible wine, and sell it. If local governments are serious about the bigger-picture economic development agenda, they will have to steer the sector in this direction.

* * *

A few weeks after the Wuzhong conference, we contacted Yanzhi on WeChat. We had heard something about a new project not far from Wuzhong but didn't know anything about it.

> I took 1100 hectares of 22-year-old vines in Ningxia [smile emoji]. A new project [smile emoji].

Really? 1,100 . . . hectares? That's more than 2,700 acres. To give you a comparison, renowned Grgich Hills in California's Napa Valley owns a grand total of 366 acres in estate vineyards. And Chateau Ste Michelle, Washington State's wine giant, owns 3,500 acres of vines in the Columbia Valley. Pierre replied,

> 1100 hectares? Not mu? You didn't type one too many zeros? [1,100 mu would be a more modest area of 73 hectares.]

Yanzhi confirmed:

> Hectares [smile emoji]. And planting 130 more hectares too. I'll show you around next time.

A year later, in 2018, we were back in Ningxia. Our trusty local taxi driver, an NBA fan, was caught in soccer World Cup fever this time. In the evening, just a block away from our hotel, an all-ages crowd gathered at outdoor tables surrounded by food vendors, in front of a big screen. They went back and forth between watching Russia play Costa Rica and admiring the impromptu dance group on the square, or taking kids to a mini rollerblading track.

In the afternoon, Pierre took the 101A bus for a quick visit to Crazy Fang at Kanaan winery. The construction was now complete, and Fang could finally live happily in her "chateau" with her husband. The downstairs part was dedicated to wine production and hosting guests. In one VIP dining room, she hosted dinners catered by a local restaurant that delivered everything. On the way to her residence upstairs, the hallway was decorated with art gathered in her travels. She had rooms for her parents too, though she told us her dad preferred to stay across the street at Helan Qingxue winery (which he'd cofounded). We sat at the round table in her living room, simply furnished with a little kitchen counter area, couch, ottoman, a treadmill, and an electric massage chair. The next day, she'd be off to Chengdu for a wine event, and then off to Shanghai for more.

While she was happy to host government officials (that seemed to be the primary purpose of the VIP dining room), media, and wine enthusiasts from time to time, Kanaan was not a tourist winery, Fang explained. You couldn't just show up and buy a ticket as you would at Changyu castles. Many people asked to visit, but she often had to decline due to lack of time and resources. It was first and foremost her house, where she lived with family and made her wine. Entering the tourism and hospitality business would require hiring specialized staff. She chose to focus on making good wine, going on the road to sell it, and spending the little free time she had relaxing at home. There are many small wineries like this all around the world, where visits are by appointment only and as the owner's availability permits. Not all wineries need to be tourist attractions.

On the wine side, big things had happened since our last visit. She no longer needed to buy grapes from farmers and relied solely on her own. One part came from her estate land around the winery, and another from "contract vineyards," which were planted just for her, managed under her supervision, and where grapes were only grown for Kanaan. She didn't have to worry about a supplier selling to a higher bidder anymore. She also had a new bottling line that put screwcaps instead of corks on her white wines. "Easier to open," she said. Screwcaps were still rare on Chinese wine bottles.

We already told you that Kanaan wines were a bit more available to consumers around China. But you could now find them in London, Switzerland, Quebec, and Australia, and she was working on a new deal with a small shop in Singapore. Another project involved an Irish Whiskey brand that released a special Silk Road label for China, aged in Kanaan red wine barrels. "I am not expanding production anymore." Fang seemed to have found a happy balance and settled in her chateau life.

The next morning, Yanzhi picked us up at our hotel. Guanlan Vineyard, now finally under construction, was just the beginning of his Ningxia wine plans. He had been thinking about doing something bigger, but there was no land available to match his ambition. Then, in 2017, he heard that a big landowner was looking to rent out one of his parcels: a thousand hectares of twenty-year-old vines (a rarity in Ningxia). The owner had even more, and in fact, the best wineries in Ningxia had been buying grapes from him for years. Yanzhi got a twenty-year lease and, on top of the existing vineyards, enough space to build a winery and plant another three hundred hectares.

We drove down an hour south of Yinchuan, on the immaculate highway G110, the one that connects other wineries up north at the foot of Helan Mountain: Chandon, Kanaan, Helan Qingxue, Yunmo, the Xixia theme park, and Guanlan, among many others. Reaching the outskirts of the city of Qingtongxia, road signs with winery names showed that the government's local wine route idea was even more ambitious than we thought, extending well beyond Yinchuan.

Yanzhi showed us around his new winery, located on a hilly spot with a small lake that, seen from above, was shaped like a bird. Overlooking the building and vineyards, there was a temple, and an ancient rock protected as a historical artifact. Yanzhi called the winery Xige Estate in English. *Xi* is for "west," and *ge* means "dove" or "pigeon," to evoke the hill's lake. Unlike at Guanlan, the construction permit came quickly. State-of-the-art equipment was installed in time for the inaugural 2017 vintage. By October 2017, Xige Estate's first wines were underway. The team could experiment with tanks of various sizes. Some could handle larger volumes for midlevel-quality wines, while smaller ones would be used for the top bottlings. Thanks to technology from New Zealand, Yanzhi could operate several functions from a phone app, such as adjusting the temperature of various tanks or setting up the times when red wines would be pumped over from the bottom to the top to submerge the cap of grape skins. Even the floors, of German design, were modern. While many other wineries used cement, here the floors were the kind you find at companies like Coca-Cola, preventing mold and keeping you worry free for a couple of decades, Yanzhi explained. Upstairs, four young women, all graduates from wine programs at Ningxia University, were analyzing samples in the in-house lab.

There were many good-quality Ningxia wines by now, but they were often the product of boutique operations with high prices that were not always competitive with imports. At Xige Estate, Yanzhi wanted to produce quality wines at prices matching their foreign peers. He counted on an astounding capacity, ten million bottles per year, combined with good equipment and a strong team, to make this possible. As often in the region, most of the old vineyard was planted with Cabernet Sauvignon. But there was also Merlot, Chardonnay, Sauvignon Blanc, Marselan, Ital-

Zhang Yanzhi explains his high-tech choices.

ian Riesling, and even Pinot Noir. He also planted the aromatic white
variety Gewurztraminer, which he thought could sell very well in China:
"It will be my nuclear weapon in a few years," he said. The bottling line
arrived a few weeks after our visit. By August 2018, just eleven months
after it all began, it was ready for the first batch: a whopping 1.2 million

bottles. A few of Yanzhi's winemaker friends from around the world came to contribute their perspectives on blending. Teamwork shaped the style of Xige Estate wines.

By 2019, the winery was fully built, complete with a large reception and tasting room area. Yanzhi also built fifty rooms, half for staff to live in and the rest open to visitors. A restaurant with vineyard and mountain views was ready to serve local food. To make all this happen so fast, Yanzhi rented an apartment in Ningxia, to spend time nurturing good relationships, but it meant only enjoying family time in Beijing a few times a month. His associates were taking care of daily operations at Easy Cellar, his Beijing wine import company. Do you remember Liao, Yanzhi's young enologist we first met at Guanlan? He did a lot of heavy lifting at Xige Estate, at a very busy time of his life. He'd just married his girlfriend Erica in 2017. The wedding took place at Changyu Moser, the Renaissance castle where you could dream of France. And soon, the couple had a daughter. So, Liao's life had been busy, between a baby and handling both Guanlan up north and Xige to the south.

Compared to Guanlan, where construction took so long to begin and, until recently, Liao had to struggle to buy in grapes and rent space from another winery to make the wines, the fast progress at Xige Estate must have been satisfying. It helped that government support was strong, but there remained open questions for Yanzhi. How many quality tiers and price points should there be? What was the right labeling strategy? Another friend, a Chinese artist who studied in France, was invited to provide a critical look at draft labels. He couldn't neglect any detail.

Going this big to build a completely new brand in lesser-known wine territory was an innovative but risky (and expensive) bet. Yanzhi's longstanding success, after all, had been to sell imports, not wine made in China. And he knew too well the difficulties many of his Ningxia peers faced. He started planting the seeds of his Ningxia wine marketing through his distribution networks for imported wine. At one dinner, he put an unmarked bottle next to Australian Penfolds and French Les Dauphins, two brands sold by his Easy Cellar import company. "This one is from Ningxia," he told the audience, inviting comments. Diners didn't take long to finish the secret bottles, giving him some confidence that his existing distributors would be willing to take on the challenge of selling Chinese wine. A few months later, Yanzhi finally bottled his first line of Xige wines with three distinct tiers: the flagship Xige Estate wine, followed by Jade Dove (with a dove on the label) and the entry-level, named after the mountain, Helan Red.

* * *

"Oooh . . . eww! Eww!" We will never forget our friend Mike's face when, right around Christmas 2012, we served him the Chardonnay that we had just flown back from Ho Chi Minh City. With Pierre's family heritage, this book could have been about the wines of Vietnam. It was too early to get into Vietnamese wine, but it was the first time we began to connect our taste for wine with our academic interests in economic development. One thing led to another, and now, here we are suggesting you begin your own Chinese wine adventure. We wrote these lines from Ho Chi Minh City, where we spent time with our two-year-old niece Isabelle, who was starting to make sentences in French and English. We couldn't help but check the wine department at a local supermarket. Chateau Dalat was there, a new label by the same producer who made the Chardonnay that overwhelmed Mike's senses. We bought the Cabernet Sauvignon and the Merlot. Were they great wines? No. But perfectly drinkable? Yes. They'd come a long, long way. Before heading back home to our basement wine rack full of Chinese wines, we stopped by Hong Kong for a little wine shopping. This time, we focused on non-Chinese wines (shocking, we know): Indonesia, Japan, Thailand, and India—it was time to discover other wines of Asia. And we heard there was wine tourism too. Asian wines . . . who would have thought?

NOTES

1. FROM CHINA TO BORDEAUX . . .
AND BACK

1. Jancis Robinson, "Chinese Wine: Catching Up Fast," *Jancis Robinson* (blog), April 4, 2014, https://www.jancisrobinson.com.

2. Victoria Moore, "A Bottle of Beijing, Please: Is Chinese Wine Any Good?" *Telegraph*, April 28, 2015, https://www.telegraph.co.uk.

3. Jim Boyce, "China Wineaversary: Grape Wall Turns Ten Today," *Grape Wall of China* (blog), June 29, 2017, http://www.grapewallofchina.com; Jim Boyce, "Decanter Magazine and Jia Bei Lan 2009: Was It Really Chinese Wine?" *Grape Wall of China* (blog), October 30, 2011, http://www. grapewallofchina.com.

4. Jamie Goode, "I've Deleted the Chinese Wine Post," *Jamie Goode's Wine Blog* (blog), October 1, 2011, http://www.wineanorak.com.

5. Jim Boyce, "China Wineaversary: Grape Wall Turns Ten Today," *Grape Wall of China* (blog), June 29, 2017, http://www.grapewallofchina.com.

6. Consumption numbers typically come from trade statistics, so experts have questioned whether folks are always drinking what they buy, but the numbers are large nonetheless. International Organisation of Vine and Wine (OIV), "Statistical Report on World Vitiviniculture 2017," International Organisation of Wine and Vine, 2017, http://www.oiv.int.

7. The 2015 data are reported here: World Wine Trade Group, "Wine Industry Overview," November 2017, https://www.trade.gov.

8. World Health Organization, *Global Status Report on Alcohol and Health, 2014* (Geneva: Author, 2014).

9. Jessica Elgot, "Woman Downs Whole Bottle of Cognac at Beijing Airport Security Control," *Guardian*, August 25, 2015, http://www.theguardian.com.

10. Adam Thomson, "Rémy Cointreau Profit Falls as China Gives Up Gifts," *Financial Times*, November 27, 2014, https://www.ft.com.

11. Jessica Beaton, "Chinese Wines Are 'Average' . . . Let's Break Out the Champagne!" *CNN Travel*, February 7, 2011, http://travel.cnn.com; Jim Boyce, "Not Bad: Robert Parker Site Ranks 18 of 20 Chinese Wines as 'Average' to 'Good,'" *Grape Wall of China* (blog), January 28, 2011, http://www.grapewallofchina.com.

12. See Jonathan Napack and *International Herald Tribune*, "China Toasts Fledgling Wineries," *New York Times*, October 15, 1999, https://www.nytimes.com; Nic Cavell, "How China Conquered France's Wine Country," *New Republic*, November 24, 2015, https://newrepublic.com; Suzanne Mustacich, *Thirsty Dragon: China's Lust for Bordeaux and the Threat to the World's Best Wines* (New York: Henry Holt, 2015).

13. This gem is from the 2013 Gaokao in Hubei Province. For more, check out Bridgett O'Donnell, "30 Absolutely Insane Questions from China's Gaokao," *That's Online*, June 7, 2018, http://www.thatsmags.com.

14. Nancy Qian and Jaya Wen, "The Impact of Xi Jinping's Anti-Corruption Campaign on Luxury Imports in China" (preliminary draft, Yale University, 2015).

15. Darren Smith, "Demand for WSET Courses Hits Record High," *Imbibe* (blog), August 4, 2017, http://imbibe.com.

16. See *Al Jazeera*'s feature on the village here: Dave Tacon, "In Pictures: China's Village of Salt," *Al Jazeera*, December 11, 2013, https://www.aljazeera.com.

2. SEA, SAND, AND SHANDONG

1. His employment contract, in English, is an auction item at Christie's. See Christie's, "Wine in China," January 16, 2014, https://www.christies.com.

2. Michael R. Godley, *The Mandarin-Capitalists from Nanyang: Overseas Chinese Enterprise in the Modernisation of China 1893–1911* (Cambridge: Cambridge University Press, 2002); Jonathan Ray, "Wine: Is China the New Chile When It Comes to Wine?," *Telegraph*, January 18, 2008, https://www.telegraph.co.uk.

3. See Baek's victory shot here: PGA Tour, "Todd Baek Cruises to Victory at Chateau Junding Penglai Open," September 8, 2014, https://www.pgatour.com.

4. Jim Boyce, "The RMB27998 Wine Question in China: Chateau Junding," *Grape Wall of China* (blog), April 2, 2011, http://www.grapewallofchina.com.

5. Jim Boyce and Bob Wise, "On the Wine Path in Shandong: Visits to Huadong, Changyu-Castel, and Chateau Junding," *Grape Wall of China* (blog), September 4, 2008, http://www.grapewallofchina.com.

6. *Global Golf Post*, "NEWS: PGA Tour China Can't Get Tournaments Approved," April 28, 2017, http://www.globalgolfpost.com; James Porteus, "Why Golf Suddenly Looks to Be in Favour in China Once Again—and How Asian Tour Can Cash In," *South China Morning News*, March 25, 2017, https://www.scmp.com; Neil Connor, "China Driving against 'Millionaire's Sport' with Closure of 100 Golf Courses," *Telegraph*, January 23, 2017, https://www.telegraph.co.uk.

7. Chris Ruffle, *A Decent Bottle of Wine in China* (New York: Earnshaw Books, 2015).

3. THE REVENGE OF THE XIXIA

1. Mike Veseth, "Washington's Invisible Vineyard: Yakima," *Wine Economist* (blog), August 20, 2013, https://wineeconomist.com.

2. Sylvia Wu, "Ningxia Announces Wine Classification System," *Decanter China*, February 16, 2016, https://www.decanterchina.com.

3. Wine Institute, "Code of Advertising Standards," June 2011, https://www.wineinstitute.org.

4. TAI DUO LE! TOO MANY!

1. See NPR's feature story, David Kestenbaum and Jacob Goldstein, "The Secret Document That Transformed China," NPR, *All Things Considered*, January 20, 2012, https://www.npr.org.

2. John McMillan, John Whalley, and Lijing Zhu, "The Impact of China's Economic Reforms on Agricultural Productivity Growth," *Journal of Political Economy* 97, no. 4 (1989): 781–807.

3. See, for example, Iain Fraser, "The Role of Contracts in Wine Grape Supply Coordination: An Overview," *Australasian Agribusiness Review* 11, no. 1673-2016-136814 (2003); and Marta Fernández Olmos, "Why Use Contracts in Viticulture?" *Journal of Wine Research* 19, no. 2 (2008): 81–93.

4. Hongdong Guo and Robert W. Jolly, "Contractual Arrangements and Enforcement in Transition Agriculture: Theory and Evidence from China," *Food*

Policy 33, no. 6 (December 2008): 570–75, https://doi.org/10.1016/j.foodpol.
2008.04.003.

5. This image and the diversity of Ningxia wine are described with remarkable depth in this *New Yorker* feature: Jiayang Fan, "Can Wine Transform China's Countryside?" March 5, 2018, https://www.newyorker.com.

6. The first is by Tim Atkin, in the *Observer* (1996). The second is by
Thomas Matthews in *Wine Spectator*, in 1995. And the last one is by *Wine
Spectator*'s James Molesworth, as late as November 2005!

7. Ian Mount, *The Vineyard at the End of the World: Maverick Winemakers
and the Rebirth of Malbec* (New York: Norton, 2012), 255.

5. FOR RENT

1. WAPA: The World Apple and Pear Association, http://www.wapa-
association.org (accessed May 24, 2019).

2. Sachiko Miyata, Nicholas Minot, and Dinghuan Hu, "Impact of Contract
Farming on Income: Linking Small Farmers, Packers, and Supermarkets in China," *World Development* 37, no. 11 (November 2009): 1781–90, https://doi.org/
10.1016/j.worlddev.2008.08.025.

3. Songqing Jin and Klaus Deininger, "Land Rental Markets in the Process
of Rural Structural Transformation: Productivity and Equity Impacts from China," *Journal of Comparative Economics* 37, no. 4 (December 2009): 629–46,
https://doi.org/10.1016/j.jce.2009.04.005.

4. Chris Ruffle, *A Decent Bottle of Wine in China* (New York: Earnshaw
Books, 2015).

5. The government agency is the Yellow River Conservancy Commission.
For more on its challenges, see Scott Moore, "The Politics of Thirst," 2014, http:/
/belfercenter.hks.harvard.edu.

6. Scott Moore, "China's Massive Water Problem," *New York Times*, October 19, 2018, https://www.nytimes.com; Jing Li, "Ningxia's Coal and Farm Projects Pose Critical Threat to Water Supplies," *South China Morning Post*, September 12, 2012, https://www.scmp.com.

7. See the project documents here: Asian Development Bank, "Project
Agreement for Ningxia Irrigated Agriculture and Water Conservation Demonstration Project," May 7, 2013, https://www.adb.org.

8. Thomas Cliff, "The Partnership of Stability in Xinjiang: State-Society
Interactions Following the July 2009 Unrest," *China Journal*, no. 68 (2012):
79–105.

9. Wei Shan and Gang Chen, "The Urumqi Riots and China's Ethnic Policy
in Xinjiang," *East Asian Policy* 1, no. 3 (2011): 14–22.

10. Government of China, "IX. Establishment, Development and Role of Xin-jiang Production and Construction Corps," May 26, 2003, http://www.china.org.cn.

11. World Bank, "Conserving Water in China's Hottest and Driest Place," World Bank, November 20, 2013, http://www.worldbank.org.

12. Jeremy Page, "China Officials Push Water Plan," *Wall Street Journal*, November 9, 2010, https://www.wsj.com.

13. CCTV International, "Chinese President Visits Anhui to Inspect Rural Reform and Development," October 1, 2008, http://www.cctv.com.

14. Lanchih Po, "Redefining Rural Collectives in China: Land Conversion and the Emergence of Rural Shareholding Co-operatives," *Urban Studies* 45, no. 8 (2008): 1603–23.

15. Richard Silk, "Could China's Farmers Become Landowners?" *Wall Street Journal*, November 8, 2013, https://www.wsj.com.

6. BACK TO SCHOOL

1. Stefano Ponte and Joachim Ewert, "Which Way Is 'Up' in Upgrading? Trajectories of Change in the Value Chain for South African Wine," *World Development* 37, no. 10 (October 2009): 1637–50, https://doi.org/10.1016/j.worlddev.2009.03.008; Evert-Jan Visser and Peter de Langen, "The Importance and Quality of Governance in the Chilean Wine Industry," *GeoJournal* 65, no. 3 (March 2006): 177–97, https://doi.org/10.1007/s10708-006-0035-8; Jane Anson, "Pascal Ribereau-Gayon Dies," *Decanter*, May 24, 2011, https://www.decanter.com.

7. SUPERPOWERED GRAPES AND SUPERHERO WINEMAKERS

1. The quotes in this paragraph are from scenes in the 2013 documentary *Red Obsession*. Warwick Ross, *Red Obsession*, DVD (Hong Kong, 2013).

2. Sylvia Wu, "Searching for China's Signature Wine Grape," *Decanter China*, May 31, 2016, https://www.decanterchina.com.

3. Cabernet Gernischt is discussed in detail on most relevant websites, including Jancis Robinson, Jim Boyce, *Decanter China*, and more.

4. Read about some of his contributions on the Chinese site, Baidu, "Guo Qichang" (Chrome will automatically translate the Chinese), https://baike.baidu.com/item/%E9%83%AD%E5%85%B6%E6%98%8C (accessed July 19, 2018);

China Wine News, "Sadly Mourning Chinese Wine Master Guo Qichang," December 21, 2015, http://www.cnwinenews.com.

5. Björn Kjellgren, "Drunken Modernity: Wine in China," *Anthropology of Food*, no. 3 (December 1, 2004), http://journals.openedition.org.

6. *Wine Spectator*, "André Tchelistcheff, 1901–1994," May 15, 1994, https://www.winespectator.com.

7. See Gadd's interview here: Declan Bush, "Winemaker Jets to China for Challenge," *Press Reader: Augusta Margaret River Times*, January 15, 2016, https://www.pressreader.com.

8. THE MOUNTAIN GUIDE

1. Matt Schiavenza, "China's Brand-New, Centuries-Old Shangri-La," *Atlantic*, January 14, 2014, https://www.theatlantic.com; David Leveille, "Shangri-La Is No More, after a Massive Fire Devastates an Ancient Tibetan Village," Public Radio International, January 13, 2014, https://www.pri.org.

2. Francis Khek Gee Lim, *Christianity in Contemporary China: Socio-Cultural Perspectives*, vol. 5 (New York: Routledge, 2013).

3. Fei Sun and Brendan Galipeau, "Inheriting Winemaking: Cizhong 'Rose Honey' Wine Production on the Upper Mekong River in Northwest Yunnan Province, China," *Himalaya: The Journal of the Association for Nepal and Himalayan Studies* 36, no. 1 (2016), https://himalayajournal.org.

4. Xianyi Xiao, "A Poacher Turned Ranger Hunts the Hunters," *China Daily*, October 10, 2012, http://www.chinadaily.com.cn.

5. Brendan A. Galipeau, "Terroir in Tibet: Wine Production, Identity, and Landscape Change in Shangri-La, China," PhD diss., University of Hawai'i at Manoa, 2017.

6. Brendan A. Galipeau, "Balancing Income, Food Security, and Sustainability in Shangri-la: The Dilemma of Monocropping Wine Grapes in Rural China," *Culture, Agriculture, Food and Environment* 37, no. 2 (2015): 74–83.

7. Jane Anson, "Anson on Thursday: Vineyards on the Roof of the World," *Decanter*, April 30, 2015, http://www.decanter.com.

8. Jancis Robinson, "China's New Wine Frontier," *Jancis Robinson* (blog), June 21, 2014, https://www.jancisrobinson.com.

9. Anson, "Anson on Thursday."

9. BUBBLY ON THE ROCKS

1. Courtney Abernathy, "Press Release: China's Imported Wine Market," *Wine Intelligence*, July 4, 2018, https://www.wineintelligence.com.

2. Bloomberg News, "Rothschild Begins Building First Lafite Asian Winery in China," *BusinessWeek: Undefined*, March 13, 2012, http://www.businessweek.com.

3. Moët & Chandon, "Moët & Chandon Celebrates Heritage in China with 'Tribute to the Spirit of 1743,'" September 6, 2011, https://www.prnewswire.co.uk. See the video on YouTube: "Hot Air Moet & Chandon Breathtaking Flight above the Great Wall of China."

4. Jeannie Cho-Lee, "Does Champagne Have a Sparkling Future in China?" Wine-Searcher, July 29, 2013, https://www.wine-searcher.com.

5. Fengye Yang, "China Food and Drinks Fair Index Top 20 Wine Brands," Wines Info, November 4, 2014, http://en.winesinfo.com.

6. Phil Mooney, "Bite the Wax Tadpole?" Coca-Cola Company, March 6, 2008, http://www.coca-colacompany.com.

7. John Pasden, "Jacob's Creek," *Sinosplice* (blog), June 25, 2006, http://www.sinosplice.com.

8. Justin Bergman, "Djokovic Caps Successful China Swing with Shanghai Title," Associated Press, October 18, 2015, https://apnews.com.

9. Wine-Searcher, "Tasting Notes: Domaine Helan Mountain Special Reserve Chardonnay, Ningxia, China," https://www.wine-searcher.com (accessed December 15, 2017).

10. FILLING OUR WINE SUITCASE

1. Jim Boyce, "Family Man in Beijing: Miguel Torres on Parker, Cava and Chinese Vineyards," *Grape Wall of China* (blog), March 6, 2013, http://www.grapewallofchina.com.

2. Jean-Baptiste Ancelot, "Emma Gao: Grande Dame of Silver Heights," *Drinks Business* (blog), October 29, 2014, https://www.thedrinksbusiness.com.

3. Jim Boyce, "Beijing's China Wine Shop: Get Kanaan Wines at Rmb100 This Saturday," *Grape Wall of China* (blog), April 9, 2015, http://www.grapewallofchina.com.

4. Harvard Business School did a long interview about his career: Harvard Business School, "Andrónico Luksic Craig: Creating Emerging Markets," https://www.hbs.edu (accessed July 19, 2018).

5. Adil Husein, "Domestic Firms Shouldn't Wait for Beijing to Act on Food Safety," *China Economic Review* (blog), July 7, 2013, https://chinaeconomicreview.com.

11. COMING TO AMERICA

1. You can find a list of their products online at http://cohoimports.com.

2. Colleen DeBaise, "The Challenges of Starting an Urban Winery," *You're the Boss Blog* (blog), June 25, 2014, https://boss.blogs.nytimes.com.

12. WHAT'S NEXT?

1. For more on this, see Peilin Li and Xiaoyi Wang, eds., *Ecological Migration, Development and Transformation: A Study of Migration and Poverty Reduction in Ningxia* (Heidelberg, Germany: Springer, 2015).

BIBLIOGRAPHY

Abernathy, Courtney. "Press Release: China's Imported Wine Market." *Wine Intelligence*, July 4, 2018. https://www.wineintelligence.com.

Ancelot, Jean-Baptiste. "Emma Gao: Grande Dame of Silver Heights." *Drinks Business* (blog), October 29, 2014. https://www.thedrinksbusiness.com.

Anson, Jane. "Anson on Thursday: Vineyards on the Roof of the World." *Decanter*, April 30, 2015. http://www.decanter.com.

———. "Pascal Ribereau-Gayon Dies." *Decanter*, May 24, 2011. https://www.decanter.com.

Asian Development Bank. "Project Agreement for Ningxia Irrigated Agriculture and Water Conservation Demonstration Project." May 7, 2013. https://www.adb.org.

Baidu. "Guo Qichang." Accessed July 19, 2018. https://baike.baidu.com/item/%E9%83%AD%E5%85%B6%E6%98%8C.

Beaton, Jessica. "Chinese Wines Are 'Average' . . . Let's Break Out the Champagne!" *CNN Travel*, February 7, 2011. http://travel.cnn.com.

Bergman, Justin. "Djokovic Caps Successful China Swing with Shanghai Title." Associated Press, October 18, 2015. https://apnews.com.

Bloomberg News. "Rothschild Begins Building First Lafite Asian Winery in China." *Business-Week: Undefined*, March 13, 2012. http://www.businessweek.com.

Boyce, Jim. "Beijing's China Wine Shop: Get Kanaan Wines at Rmb100 This Saturday." *Grape Wall of China* (blog), April 9, 2015. http://www.grapewallofchina.com.

———. "China Wineaversary: Grape Wall Turns Ten Today." *Grape Wall of China* (blog), June 29, 2017. http://www.grapewallofchina.com.

———. "China Wine Word: Decanter's Sarah Kemp Reflects on Jia Bei Lan Brouhaha." *Grape Wall of China* (blog), February 28, 2012. http://www.grapewallofchina.com.

———. "Decanter Magazine and Jia Bei Lan 2009: Was It Really Chinese Wine?" *Grape Wall of China* (blog), October 30, 2011. http://www.grapewallofchina.com.

———. "Family Man in Beijing: Miguel Torres on Parker, Cava and Chinese Vineyards." *Grape Wall of China* (blog), March 6, 2013. http://www.grapewallofchina.com.

———. "Not Bad: Robert Parker Site Ranks 18 of 20 Chinese Wines as 'Average' to 'Good.'" *Grape Wall of China* (blog), January 28, 2011. http://www.grapewallofchina.com.

———. "The RMB27998 Wine Question in China: Chateau Junding." *Grape Wall of China* (blog), April 2, 2011. http://www.grapewallofchina.com.

Boyce, Jim, and Bob Wise. "On the Wine Path in Shandong: Visits to Huadong, Changyu-Castel, and Chateau Junding." *Grape Wall of China* (blog), September 4, 2008. http://www.grapewallofchina.com.

Bush, Declan. "Winemaker Jets to China for Challenge." *Press Reader: Augusta Margaret River Times*, January 15, 2016. https://www.pressreader.com.

Cavell, Nic. "How China Conquered France's Wine Country." *New Republic*, November 24, 2015. https://newrepublic.com.

CCTV International. "Chinese President Visits Anhui to Inspect Rural Reform and Development." October 1, 2008. http://www.cctv.com.

China Wine News. "Sadly Mourning Chinese Wine Master Guo Qichang." December 21, 2015. http://www.cnwinenews.com.

Cho-Lee, Jeannie. "Does Champagne Have a Sparkling Future in China?" Wine-Searcher, July 29, 2013. https://www.wine-searcher.com.

Christie's. "Wine in China." January 16, 2014. https://www.christies.com.

Cliff, Thomas. "The Partnership of Stability in Xinjiang: State-Society Interactions Following the July 2009 Unrest." *China Journal*, no. 68 (2012): 79–105.

Connor, Neil. "China Driving against 'Millionaire's Sport' with Closure of 100 Golf Courses." *Telegraph*, January 23, 2017. https://www.telegraph.co.uk.

DeBaise, Colleen. "The Challenges of Starting an Urban Winery." *You're the Boss Blog* (blog), June 25, 2014. https://boss.blogs.nytimes.com.

Elgot, Jessica. "Woman Downs Whole Bottle of Cognac at Beijing Airport Security Control." *Guardian*, August 25, 2015. http://www.theguardian.com.

Fan, Jiayang. "Can Wine Transform China's Countryside?" March 5, 2018. https://www.newyorker.com.

Fraser, Iain. "The Role of Contracts in Wine Grape Supply Coordination: An Overview." *Australasian Agribusiness Review* 11, no. 1673-2016-136814 (2003).

Galipeau, Brendan A. "Balancing Income, Food Security, and Sustainability in Shangri-La: The Dilemma of Monocropping Wine Grapes in Rural China." *Culture, Agriculture, Food and Environment* 37, no. 2 (2015): 74–83.

———. "Terroir in Tibet: Wine Production, Identity, and Landscape Change in Shangri-La, China." PhD diss., University of Hawai'i at Manoa, 2017.

Global Golf Post. "NEWS: PGA Tour China Can't Get Tournaments Approved." April 28, 2017. http://www.globalgolfpost.com.

Godley, Michael R. *The Mandarin-Capitalists from Nanyang: Overseas Chinese Enterprise in the Modernisation of China, 1893–1911*. Cambridge: Cambridge University Press, 2002.

Goode, Jamie. "I've Deleted the Chinese Wine Post." *Jamie Goode's Wine Blog* (blog), October 1, 2011. http://www.wineanorak.com.

Government of China. "IX. Establishment, Development and Role of Xinjiang Production and Construction Corps." May 26, 2003. http://www.china.org.cn.

Guo, Hongdong, and Robert W. Jolly. "Contractual Arrangements and Enforcement in Transition Agriculture: Theory and Evidence from China." *Food Policy* 33, no. 6 (December 2008): 570–75. https://doi.org/10.1016/j.foodpol.2008.04.003.

Harvard Business School. "Andrónico Luksic Craig: Creating Emerging Markets." Accessed July 19, 2018. https://www.hbs.edu.

Husein, Adil. "Domestic Firms Shouldn't Wait for Beijing to Act on Food Safety." *China Economic Review* (blog), July 7, 2013. https://chinaeconomicreview.com.

International Organisation of Vine and Wine (OIV). "OIV's Focus on the Sparkling Wine Market." October 11, 2014. http://www.oiv.int.

———. "Statistical Report on World Vitiviniculture 2017." http://www.oiv.int.

Jin, Songqing, and Klaus Deininger. "Land Rental Markets in the Process of Rural Structural Transformation: Productivity and Equity Impacts from China." *Journal of Comparative Economics* 37, no. 4 (December 2009): 629–46. https://doi.org/10.1016/j.jce.2009.04.005.

Kestenbaum, David, and Jacob Goldstein. "The Secret Document That Transformed China." NPR. *All Things Considered*. January 20, 2012. https://www.npr.org.

Kjellgren, Björn. "Drunken Modernity: Wine in China." *Anthropology of Food*, no. 3 (December 1, 2004). http://journals.openedition.org.

Leveille, David. "Shangri-La Is No More, after a Massive Fire Devastates an Ancient Tibetan Village." Public Radio International. January 13, 2014. https://www.pri.org.

Li, Jing. "Ningxia's Coal and Farm Projects Pose Critical Threat to Water Supplies." *South China Morning Post*, September 12, 2012. https://www.scmp.com.

Li, Peilin, and Xiaoyi Wang, eds. *Ecological Migration, Development and Transformation: A Study of Migration and Poverty Reduction in Ningxia.* Heidelberg, Germany: Springer, 2015.

Lim, Francis Khek Gee. *Christianity in Contemporary China: Socio-Cultural Perspectives.* Vol. 5. New York: Routledge, 2013.

McMillan, John, John Whalley, and Lijing Zhu. "The Impact of China's Economic Reforms on Agricultural Productivity Growth." *Journal of Political Economy* 97, no. 4 (1989): 781–807.

Miyata, Sachiko, Nicholas Minot, and Dinghuan Hu. "Impact of Contract Farming on Income: Linking Small Farmers, Packers, and Supermarkets in China." *World Development* 37, no. 11 (November 2009): 1781–90. https://doi.org/10.1016/j.worlddev.2008.08.025.

Moët & Chandon. "Moët & Chandon Celebrates Heritage in China with 'Tribute to the Spirit of 1743.'" September 6, 2011. https://www.prnewswire.co.uk.

Mooney, Phil. "Bite the Wax Tadpole?" Coca-Cola Company, March 6, 2008. http://www.coca-colacompany.com.

Moore, Scott. "China's Massive Water Problem." *New York Times*, October 19, 2018. https://www.nytimes.com.

———. "The Politics of Thirst." 2014. http://belfercenter.hks.harvard.edu.

Moore, Victoria. "A Bottle of Beijing, Please: Is Chinese Wine Any Good?" *Telegraph*, April 28, 2015. https://www.telegraph.co.uk.

Mount, Ian. *The Vineyard at the End of the World: Maverick Winemakers and the Rebirth of Malbec.* New York: Norton, 2012.

Mustacich, Suzanne. *Thirsty Dragon: China's Lust for Bordeaux and the Threat to the World's Best Wines.* New York: Henry Holt, 2015.

Napack, Jonathan, and *International Herald Tribune.* "China Toasts Fledgling Wineries." *New York Times*, October 15, 1999. https://www.nytimes.com.

O'Donnell, Bridgett. "30 Absolutely Insane Questions from China's Gaokao." *That's Online*, June 7, 2018. http://www.thatsmags.com.

Olmos, Marta Fernández. "Why Use Contracts in Viticulture?" *Journal of Wine Research* 19, no. 2 (2008): 81–93.

Page, Jeremy. "China Officials Push Water Plan." *Wall Street Journal*, November 9, 2010. https://www.wsj.com.

Pasden, John. "Jacob's Creek." *Sinosplice* (blog), June 25, 2006. http://www.sinosplice.com.

PGA Tour. "Todd Baek Cruises to Victory at Chateau Junding Penglai Open." September 8, 2014. https://www.pgatour.com.

Po, Lanchih. "Redefining Rural Collectives in China: Land Conversion and the Emergence of Rural Shareholding Co-operatives." *Urban Studies* 45, no. 8 (2008): 1603–23.

Ponte, Stefano, and Joachim Ewert. "Which Way Is 'Up' in Upgrading? Trajectories of Change in the Value Chain for South African Wine." *World Development* 37, no. 10 (October 2009): 1637–50. https://doi.org/10.1016/j.worlddev.2009.03.008.

Porteus, James. "Why Golf Suddenly Looks to Be in Favour in China Once Again—and How Asian Tour Can Cash In." *South China Morning News*, March 25, 2017. https://www.scmp.com.

Qian, Nancy, and Jaya Wen. "The Impact of Xi Jinping's Anti-Corruption Campaign on Luxury Imports in China." Preliminary draft, Yale University, 2015.

Ray, Jonathan. "Wine: Is China the New Chile When It Comes to Wine?" *Telegraph*, January 18, 2008. https://www.telegraph.co.uk.

Robinson, Jancis. "China's New Wine Frontier." *Jancis Robinson* (blog), June 21, 2014. https://www.jancisrobinson.com.

———. "Chinese Wine: Catching Up Fast." *Jancis Robinson* (blog), April 4, 2014. https://www.jancisrobinson.com.

Ross, Warwick. *Red Obsession.* DVD. Hong Kong, 2013.

Ruffle, Chris. *A Decent Bottle of Wine in China.* New York: Earnshaw Books, 2015.

Schiavenza, Matt. "China's Brand-New, Centuries-Old Shangri-La." *Atlantic*, January 14, 2014. https://www.theatlantic.com.

Shan, Wei, and Gang Chen. "The Urumqi Riots and China's Ethnic Policy in Xinjiang." *East Asian Policy* 1, no. 3 (2011): 14–22.

Silk, Richard. "Could China's Farmers Become Landowners?" *Wall Street Journal*, November 8, 2013. https://www.wsj.com.

Smith, Darren. "Demand for WSET Courses Hits Record High." *Imbibe* (blog), August 4, 2017. http://imbibe.com.

Sun, Fei, and Brendan Galipeau. "Inheriting Winemaking: Cizhong 'Rose Honey' Wine Production on the Upper Mekong River in Northwest Yunnan Province, China." *Himalaya: The Journal of the Association for Nepal and Himalayan Studies* 36, no. 1 (2016). https://himalayajournal.org.

Tacon, Dave. "In Pictures: China's Village of Salt." *Al Jazeera*, December 11, 2013. https://www.aljazeera.com.

Thomson, Adam. "Rémy Cointreau Profit Falls as China Gives Up Gifts." *Financial Times*, November 27, 2014. https://www.ft.com.

Veseth, Mike. "Washington's Invisible Vineyard: Yakima." *Wine Economist* (blog), August 20, 2013. https://wineeconomist.com.

Visser, Evert-Jan, and Peter de Langen. "The Importance and Quality of Governance in the Chilean Wine Industry." *GeoJournal* 65, no. 3 (March 2006): 177–97. https://doi.org/10.1007/s10708-006-0035-8.

Wang, Janet Z. *The Chinese Wine Renaissance: A Wine Lover's Companion*. London: Ebury Press, 2019.

WAPA: The World Apple and Pear Association. Home page. Accessed May 24, 2019. http://www.wapa-association.org.

Wine Institute. "Code of Advertising Standards." June 2011. https://www.wineinstitute.org.

Wine-Searcher. "Tasting Notes: Domaine Helan Mountain Special Reserve Chardonnay, Ningxia, China." Accessed December 15, 2017. https://www.wine-searcher.com.

Wine Spectator. "André Tchelistcheff, 1901–1994." May 15, 1994. https://www.winespectator.com.

World Bank. "Conserving Water in China's Hottest and Driest Place." November 20, 2013. http://www.worldbank.org.

World Health Organization. *Global Status Report on Alcohol and Health, 2014*. Geneva: Author, 2014.

World Wine Trade Group. "Wine Industry Overview." November 2017. https://www.trade.gov.

Wu, Sylvia. "Ningxia Announces Wine Classification System." *Decanter China*, February 16, 2016. https://www.decanterchina.com.

———. "Searching for China's Signature Wine Grape." *Decanter China*, May 31, 2016. https://www.decanterchina.com.

Xiao, Xianyi. "A Poacher Turned Ranger Hunts the Hunters." *China Daily*, October 10, 2012. http://www.chinadaily.com.cn.

Xin, Livia. "Sparkling Wine Gains Recognition in China." *Drinks Business* (blog), November 6, 2013. https://www.thedrinksbusiness.com.

Yang, Fengye. "China Food and Drinks Fair Index Top 20 Wine Brands." Wines Info, November 4, 2014. http://en.winesinfo.com.

INDEX

ABOUT THE AUTHORS

Pierre and Cynthia met in an elevator in Bangladesh in 2004. Since then, they have followed each other studying economic development and searching for new adventures in culture, food, and wine. Their work has been featured in the *Wine Economist*, the *Conversation*, and *Alternative Emerging Investor*. Find them on Instagram @cynthiapierrewine.

Cynthia Howson is senior lecturer in ethnic, gender, and labor studies at the University of Washington Tacoma. Her love of travel and asking nosy questions has allowed her to meet amazing people and tell their stories. In addition to China, her field research has taken her to Senegal, the Gambia, and the Democratic Republic of the Congo. She has a PhD from the School of Oriental and African Studies in London, UK, and a master's from Sciences Po, Bordeaux, in France.

Pierre Ly is associate professor of international political economy at the University of Puget Sound, where he teaches a popular course about the Idea of Wine. He has a PhD in economics from the Toulouse School of Economics in France. He enjoys repeatedly failing to improve his Mandarin on the internet.